Great Leaders Make for Great
Companies

THE TEN
DISCIPLINES OF
LEADERSHIP

D1546129

RICHARD A. JACOBS
AND
CHARLES B. DYGERT

Richard A. Jacobs
June. 2015

ISBN: 978-1939779-31-1 (Paperback)
ISBN: 978-1939779-32-8 (Ebook)

Published by

LIFEBRIDGE
BOOKS
P.O. Box 49428
Charlotte, NC 28277

CONTENTS

THE LEADERSHIP PLAYBOOK   5

DISCIPLINE #1: PSYCHOLOGY   11

DISCIPLINE #2: SOCIOLOGY   23

DISCIPLINE #3: PHILOSOPHY   43

DISCIPLINE #4: GEOGRAPHY   58

DISCIPLINE #5: HISTORY   73

DISCIPLINE #6: POLITICAL SCIENCE   88

DISCIPLINE #7: ECONOMICS   101

DISCIPLINE #8: ANTHROPOLOGY   116

DISCIPLINE #9: MATHEMATICS   130

DISCIPLINE #10: COMMUNICATION   143

"Rarely does a book take on two significant aspects of business—management and leadership—and craft a way to illustrate that they must each be linked in order to maximize results."
– BOB MESSAROS, PRESIDENT/CEO, COMMERCIAL METAL FORMING

"This outstanding book trains the mind of the leader to quickly assess each situation and use the social sciences like a "playbook" for results."
– AL STUEMPEL: EXECUTIVE COACH & FACILITATOR, VISTAGE INTERNATIONAL

"My 16 years as a TEC / Vistage Chair has opened my depth of learning about leadership from speakers, the members, and the experience. We are sharing some of these lessons in <u>The Ten Disciplines – The Leader's Playbook</u>."
– RICH JACOBS

THE LEADERSHIP PLAYBOOK

The legendary Notre Dame head football coach, Knute Rockne, once observed, "Four years of football are calculated to breed in the average man more of the ingredients of success in life than almost any academic course he takes."

The reason this is true, is because the ability to achieve is not the result of mastering one particular discipline, intellectually or physically. Rather, it is the art of understanding, applying, and balancing several skill sets and knowledge.

The impetus for writing this book was triggered several years ago by a comment made by business guru, Peter Drucker, when he said, "Management is a liberal art." We immediately began outlining and organizing a manuscript based on that concept.

At the time, our country was immersed in the middle of an Information Technology boom and the Gulf War to free Kuwait (1990-91) had been a short military success. Then, on that fateful day, September 11, 2001, terrorists struck our homeland and everything drastically changed.

Since then we've launched two wars in the Middle East that have dragged out over time. Politics has become more divisive, and it seems as though every issue results in "us vs. them."

- Progressives vs. conservatives
- Sunnis vs. Shiites
- Muslims vs. Christians
- Jews vs. Palestinians
- Michigan vs. Ohio State
- Blue states vs. Red states
  — and on and on.

It is into this environment that we have picked up the pieces of our original work and moved forward to present what you are holding in your hands.

Today men and women at the top of the leadership triangle are challenged with problems that are multi-faceted and often have no clear approach to address them. This book has been prepared as a "playbook" on how to tackle issues of this sort.

In the sports world, a "timeout" is often used for the coach and the team to sit down and quickly go over their alternatives from their game plan and decide what will work the best. During a theatrical play or concert, the actors and musicians hastily assess if the effects, lighting, and tone are just right for the audience. And if not, what adjustments are needed. In these times of exploding social media, politicians are seen to change direction as soon as the wind blows the other way. We live in a time of constant evaluation and decision making.

The intent of this book is to help train the thoughts of the leader to quickly assess each situation and then go through the playbook (in his/her mind).

In simple terms, here is how this might work:

1. The "difficult person" problem. Would using PSYCHOLOGY in order to evaluate the situation help?
   - Why do we look at things (behave) the way we do?
   - What forms our behavioral patterns?
   - How do our attitudes inform our actions?

2. The "toxic team" problem. SOCIOLOGY says an issue involving the group must be resolved by the group.
   - How do people behave when they work together?
   - Why are teams sometimes successful, while other times they are not?
   - What kind of structure do we need for our organization?

3. The "decision making" problem. Your personal PHILOSOPHY of leadership has a significant impact on the enterprise.
   - What is your plan, and why?
   - How do you feel about your decisions?
   - What roles do ethics and integrity play?
   - Our beliefs; where do they come from?

4. The "Not in this town" problem. This could include dealing with environmental concerns, highway right-aways, building permits, or any number of issues that touch on GEOGRAPHY.
   - What determined where we located?
   - Where is our market?
   - How do factors such as weather and logistics affect us?

5. "We have been there before and it doesn't work" problem. There are great lessons to be learned in studying the HISTORY of the world, of countries, of states, towns, and "yes" organizations. What have we overlooked that might have provided us with clues?
   - When have we been here before?
   - How did it turn out?
   - What can we learn from the past?

6. The "power" problem. POLITICAL SCIENCE has very little to do with "science" and everything to do with "power" and "politics."
   - How can a leader work with those who have differing agendas?
   - What is the right balance between authority, accountability, and a positive work environment?
   - Do our actions build the organization or promote our career?

7. The "Can we afford this?" problem. In the private sector, funds must be raised based on the probability of a return. The ECONOMICS of each project need to be carefully analyzed.
   - How much can we invest?
   - Where can we find more financial resources?
   - How much profit can we produce?

8. "The merger problem." When two organizations combine; the cultures often collide. ANTHROPOL-OGY offers us case studies of this happening.
   - Why do we operate the way we do?
   - Where did our belief systems and traditions originate?
   - Do any of our organizational habits need to be fine-tuned or changed?

9. The "Does the data make sense?" problem. As Peter Drucker says, "What gets measured gets done." For this reason, MATHEMATICS is significant.
   - How do we keep score?
   - Who is winning; who is losing?
   - Where do we stand regarding resources, quality, and market share?

10. The "listening, advising, and coaching" problem. An organization moves forward with a well-conceived COMMUNICATION plan—both internally and externally.

- How does social (instant) media affect the way our enterprise operates?
- How do we let each other know what is going on?
- Are we listening as much as we are speaking?
- Are the questions we are asking the right ones?

It is our desire that as a result of examining the principles found on these pages, you will understand how each distinct area of knowledge interrelates and impacts you and your organization.

Together, let's look at the what, when, where, why, who, and how of business and personal success. They are found in *The Ten Disciplines of Leadership.*

– Charles B. Dygert and Richard A. Jacobs

DISCIPLINE #1

PSYCHOLOGY

The beatings will stop when the morale improves.
– Sign posted on a Japanese Navy destroyer, 1945.

In our years of teaching, managing, consulting, sitting on corporate and community boards, and conducting training workshops, there are certain issues that seem to crop up constantly. They usually center around one major question: "Why do people behave the way they do?"

Far too often, the issue stems from being under the thumb of an authoritarian leader with a "my way or the highway" approach."

In our work lives, family lives, almost everywhere we turn, we find that we and others are seeking to be in charge. In fact, research confirms that the predominant style of management for the past few decades has been one of COMMAND and CONTROL.

Why do we insist on making the major decisions? Why do we find strange alliances being formed so that someone doesn't lose his or her power base? And where does democracy fit into the picture?

The phenomena is not new. Back in the first century, we learn of two enemies becoming "friends" for the sake of control, then allowing democracy to cause them to make a decision that at least one of them knew was wrong. Herod, the Roman who ruled over the Jews had been trying to kill Jesus since his birth in Bethlehem. But Pontius Pilate, the governor under Herod, did not want blood on his hands. So, the decision was made to place two prisoners, Jesus and Barabbas, before an unruly "mob" and let them decide which one should be set free. They shouted "Barabbas!"

When the going gets tough, control and command suddenly embraces democracy and lets the mob rule. This is "gutless managing." The other popular thing to do when backed into a corner is to fire someone and buy time.

For years we have learned a phrase from both the Iranians and Iraqis: "The enemy of our enemy is our friend." However, the question is: *Are we siding with one against the other or might they both gang up against America?*

So often we crave control, but we are afraid to lead! We have found, to our partial dismay, that it doesn't matter so much where you are on the corporate ladder, as long as you can stay in charge.

UNDERSTANDING OURSELVES AND OTHERS

With this as a background, to better understand why managers and leaders adopt such thinking, we turn to the first discipline: psychology. It places the focus on us as individuals and helps us to understand ourselves, our thoughts, our actions, our attitude. At the same time it enables us to better recognize those same traits in others. How do we process the questions of our feelings regarding "good" and "evil"?

If you look at dictionary definitions of psychology, you find phrases such as: "The science of the human mind in any of its aspects, powers, or functions." "The study of the thought process and behavior of humans in their interaction with their environment."

This field is concerned with the sensory, motor, thinking, and feeling processes in individual human behavior. The focus is on investigating the mechanisms of psychic behavior within the individual.

As we will see, psychology touches on many of the other disciplines we will examine, including, sociology, political science, anthropology, and communication.

When applied to the relationships of people with one another, we find the term "social psychology." Among other things, it involves the study of such processes as cooperation, competition, changes in attitude, decision making and leadership itself.

Social psychologists begin their research by developing theories—then collect evidence to support them. For example, the American social psychologist, Leon Festinger, formulated the theory that people become uneasy when they learn new information that conflicts with what they already believe. He suggested that men and women do much to avoid this uneasiness, which he called *cognitive dissonance.*

Researchers collected data showing that people who

believe they are failures often avoid successes, even when they can easily achieve them. Why? Because success would conflict with their own belief in themselves as failures.

The first textbooks on social psychology were published in the early 1900s. However, modern social psychology owes much to the behavioral psychologists of the 1930s who called for the scientific study of observable behavior. Today, social psychology continues to stress the precise measurement of people's actions.

Another major influence on social psychology was the work of George Herbert Mead and Kurt Lewin. Mead, an American psychologist and philosopher, argued that men's and women's ideas about themselves are developed through social contact. Lewin, a German-born psychologist, investigated how individuals in groups are affected by other members. Both Mead and Lewin claimed that behavior depends primarily on how men and women interpret the social world. The work of these early researchers continues to influence social psychologists, who study people's perception of themselves and others.

LAYING THE FOUNDATION

It is important to have an understanding of two major psychologists whose work laid the foundation for the continuing study of this discipline.

William James (1842-1910)

He was the son of Henry James, Sr., who had inherited a fortune from his father and emigrated from Ireland to America in 1789. Henry lived a life of religious activity, dissociated from any established church. He described himself as follows: "Say I'm a philosopher, say I'm a seeker for truth, say I'm a lover of my kind, say I'm an author of books if you like, or best of all, just say I'm a student." William's brother, Henry Jr., became a noted author.

William was trained in physiology with an interest in psychology. He wrote *The Principles of Psychology*, which was published in 1891, and he also penned *The Will to Believe and Other Essays in Popular Philosophy* in 1897. James had been concerned with religion from an empirical point of view as early as 1869. However, he lost interest in psychology and turned to philosophy; some of his principles on this topic were published after his death.

His views on *determinism* and *pragmatism* should both be studied by managers and leaders, as well as his views on religion and his research in psychology.

Abraham Harold Maslow (1908-1970)

Maslow was an American psychologist whom many consider the founder of a movement called "humanistic psychology." The movement developed as a revolt against behaviorism and psychoanalysis, the two most popular psychological views of the mid-1900s.

Humanistic psychologists believe individuals are primarily controlled by their own values and choices and not by the environment (as behaviorists think), or by unconscious drives (as psychoanalysts believe).

Maslow stressed the importance of studying well-adjusted people in society, instead of only those who were disturbed.

He identified several levels of human needs, the most basic of which must be satisfied before the next levels can be fulfilled. The primary needs are bodily driven, such as hunger and thirst. Succeeding levels include the desire for safety and love. The highest need is for the fulfillment of one's unique potential, which Maslow called self-actualization (which we will discuss later in this chapter).

In our book, *Managing for Success*, we point out Maslow's belief that "The person who tends to believe that all people are essentially good will show the same resistance to change of this belief as will the person who believes all people are essentially bad."

Elliott Jaques (1917-2003)

This Canadian born psychologist has been described as "the most undeservedly ignored management researcher of the modern era." He made a major contribution to the field with his "Stratified Systems Theory," which provides guidelines for measuring a person's potential for serving in a variety of leadership positions.

We recommend that you read his book, *Requisite Organization*. It presents his research on "time horizon." He is able to categorize us into a number of strata and shows us the impact this has on organizations. Since 10 percent of our population is unemployable, 40 percent can do *Stratum #1*

16

(work) and another 40 percent can do *Stratums #1* and *#2*, you can readily see that *Stratums #3* through *#8* contain only 10 percent of the population.

THE PATH FROM BRAWN TO BRAIN

To better understand why psychology is such an important "tool" in the toolbox of today's leader, we need to take a quick look at what has brought us to this point.

Work in the crafts or "cottage" industries prior to the industrial revolution was based on both the physical and mental efforts of individuals, families, or small groups who supported themselves by making such items as shoes, clothes, brooms, nails, candles, etc. However, with the advent of the industrial revolution, workers of different ages, skills, and backgrounds were clustered together to gain the mechanical advantage of combining the *physical effort* of more than one person. It was the "toil" that was sought; the mental potential was neither utilized nor "asked for."

Wages were paid for the pure physical effort of the people doing the work. The "best workers" were those who not only could give the most effort, but the ones who conformed (e.g. did not ask, did not cause trouble, etc.).

They were paid for the labor of their backs and the toil of their hands; not the ideas from their minds. Is it little wonder that work has been associated with drudgery? So now, all of a sudden, we are asking people to think, asking them *what* they think, etc. No wonder we have created a great deal of confusion!

Organizations that learned to gain the benefit of its members' thoughts, ideas, and innovation, as well as their physical skills, created an enthusiastic, motivated group of people—far different from those whose only experience was the "drudgery" and daily grind.

Even today's foot soldier in our modern military is asked to rely on many mental skills, as well as physical ones.

This whole "people" or "behavior" issue has become more important as this workplace evolution takes place. How many of our managers have been educated to have an awareness of it, let alone know how to deal with it? How many have been selected based on their ability to lead people by their own behavior, which in turn, can influence the actions of others?

THE RAMIFICATIONS

Psychologists study every kind of human behavior you can think of:

- People who are conscious.
- People who are unconscious.
- People who are sick.
- People who are healthy.
- People at sleep.
- People who are awake.

Those who are conscious, healthy, and wide awake spend one-third of their day at work which provides the economic means to support them and their family's total well being, unless these economics are supplemented by another source.

We need to seriously study psychology as it relates to behavior in the workplace because it has so many ramifications:

- What makes us tick?
- How can we change our own and other's behavior?
- How does behavior relate to motivation?
- Why do we shift so much from one day to another in our thoughts?
- How do we get a group of people to support one agenda—the agenda of our organization?
- Do our managers know the difference between task-oriented supervision and relationship-based managing?

BEHAVIORS LEADING TO SELF-ACTUALIZATION

There is a very significant term that continually surfaces in the writings of well-known psychologists and theorists such as Kurt Goldstein, Carl Rogers, and Maslow: *self-actualization.* It is seen as the result of our basic needs being fulfilled and we turn to "actualize" our potential. This is when we experience fully, vividly, selflessly, with full concentration and total absorption.

- Self-actualization lets us think of life as a process of choices, one after another. At each point there is either a progression or a regression choice.
- Self-actualization implies that there is a self to be actualized. We are not a lump of clay.
- Self-actualization means, when in doubt, be honest rather than not.

Far too many have experiences without self-awareness, they act on impulses rather than reason and make the easy choice rather than one that requires a challenge.

Many can tell you about "peak experiences" of self-actualization. They are the "ah ha" moments of ecstasy which cannot be bought, sought, or guaranteed. One must be, as C. S. Lewis wrote, "surprised by joy."

It is possible to have "peak experiences" as a manager or leader. They may not rise to the surface often, but they are "out there."

THE "BEING VALUES"

Abraham H. Maslow died on June 8, 1970, of a fatal heart attack. His book, *The Farther Reaches of Human Nature,* was published the next year with the permission of his wife.

In this work, the renown psychologist writes about what he calls Being-Values. He says:

Self-actualizing people are, without one single exception, involved in a cause outside their own skin, in something outside of themselves. They are devoted, working at something, something which is very precious to them—some calling or vocations in the old sense, the priestly sense. They are working at something which fate has called them to somehow and which they work at and which they love, so that the work-joy dichotomy in them disappears.

One devotes his life to the law, another to justice, another to beauty or truth. All, in one way or another, devote their lives to search for which I have called the 'being' values' ['B' for short], the ultimate values which are intrinsic, which cannot be reduced to anything more ultimate.

There are about fourteen of these B-values, including the truth and beauty and goodness of the ancients and perfection, simplicity, comprehensiveness, and several more.

Throughout his works, Maslow explores man's requirement for more "self-actualization" after his basic needs are met. However, too many times, in practice, as people in the workplace start to feel "comfortable," "creative," and "committed," the leaders try to "put the fear of God in them again" and shake things up. Is this because managers are too insecure and incompetent to build on what would appear to be a good situation?

Self-actualization is not only an end state but also the

process of actualizing one's potentialities at any time, in any amount. For example, if one is an intelligent individual, he or she makes the decision to become even smarter by studying. In other words, rather than looking at the Ten Disciplines and commenting, "that's interesting," they decide to delve into each subject with a passion and apply the knowledge they learn to the task at hand.

This is why we are asking you to make a commitment to carve out the time in your daily schedule to do more than casual reading in each of these fields of study. Then, at the right moment, when the need arises, you will be able to act on that information with knowledge, confidence, authority, and effectiveness.

Notes for your Playbook

- Leadership requires more than command and control.
- The knowledge of psychology leads to an understanding of ourselves and others.
- Psychology touches on several of the Ten Disciplines.
- Social psychology involves processes of competition, cooperation, and more.
- Every leader should have a knowledge of the writings of William James, Abraham Maslow, and others.
- How the world of work has transitioned from intensive labor to productivity through intellect.
- Understand the processes that lead to self-actualization.

DISCIPLINE #2

SOCIOLOGY

If it's far away, it's news, but
if it's close at home, it's sociology.
– James Reston

The story goes something like this.

A new leader has recently been appointed [which means that most of us did not get to vote on it]. In addition, our new "hero" got a little mixed up in the wording and heard that he/she had been "anointed" instead of "appointed."

At first, things move along rather smoothly as the chosen one acquires the trappings of power with an office, car, plane etc., which demonstrates the absolute importance of this little-known individual.

Meanwhile, "back at the shop," people continue to do what they have done for years—show up every morning, put in a good day's work, and keep the economic engine of the organization moving at full speed, thus assuring good results—which will become the property of our leader—to his/her credit.

Our recently-named commander did not realize how

good he/she was or how easy it seemed to be. Then one day, in this wonderful world, a major problem rears its ugly head. Poor service [delivery, quality, performance, communication] has impacted a major customer. Our fearless leader is now called to perform his/her magic. After all, isn't this why the person was selected?

So what happens next? Well, we now need to focus all our energy and attention to finding out who to blame. The leader knows that he/she is faultless so the mission is to uncover who messed up and fire the employee for all to see. Thus, with this demonstration of executive power, the problem is unlikely to occur again. Sure!

Unfortunately, our narcissistic leader has not been introduced to root-cause analysis. Will he/she take the time to probe, ask, listen etc., in order to find out why the customer went unsatisfied? Probably not. After all, it is the management system our new hero is tampering with that is responsible for many of our successes or failures. How will this self-anointed, self-important individual ever hope to find out what real problems exist? Chances are that he/she never will!

Does the customer care that the perceived culprit has been identified and fired? Not at all; they just want to know if the issue has been fixed so that it won't happen again.

Another of our management system components comes into play here—responsibility.

Who is ultimately responsible for seeing that our customers are delighted? Is it not our self-centered, all-important hero—the leader? Sometimes our own self-admiration masks our ability to see or know just who really is paramount.

The narcissistic leader has been self-taught to believe that he/she is highest on the totem pole. Within this framework, how can customers, shareholders, employees, suppliers, communities, lien holders, and other parts of the vital overall organizational community [known as stakeholders] hope to feel that they are number one? They won't because they aren't!

Our next management system component is accountability. Who is holding our narcissistic leader answerable? No one—if he/she can help it. Self-accountability gets intermixed with self-importance so the charge is passed on to others, whether they have the responsibility, authority or not. The delusion of "self-love" has helped to make our ego-driven leader hold him/herself blameless.

"THE QUEEN OF SCIENCES"

When we look at the dynamics of the group over which this leader is presiding, we have discovered SOCIOLOGY.

This discipline was given its name by a French philosopher, August Comte, over a century ago. It was his prophetic vision that sociology was destined to be the "queen of the sciences" and so it is.

Sociology can be defined as the systematic study of human social relations. The initial image created by this definition is one of an active process of inquiry. Both anthropologists and sociologists collect information about people by living among them, i.e., by "participant observation." However, there are times when it is not possible or necessary to participate in the behavior that is being observed.

To better understand how the social system is interrelated with management, behavioral, and technical systems, here's how productivity guru J. A. Edosomwan illustrates it in his excellent *Organizational and Process Transformation Model.*

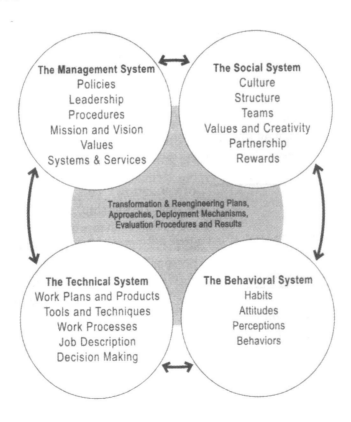

In an organization, sociology is an extension of personal relationships into groups; the "invention" and structure of teams fits here.

It's essential to see how the first of our two disciplines, psychology and sociology, are related. Our one-on-one interactions involve relationships between two people—and is in the realm of psychology. But when we look at how an organization is structured, and "group dynamics"—internally and externally—we are dealing with sociology.

In this process we discover there are many variances among people groups due to any number of "background factors." We often refer to this as our *cultural differences.* For example, what is considered a compliment in one society may be an insult in another.

In our global economy (1) *we* are going there, (2) *they* are coming here, and (3) a number of groups are continuing to disperse themselves "*among us.*"

An insightful book by professor Joel Kotkin, *Tribes: How Race, Religion, and Identity Determine Success in the New Global Economy,* is an excellent source of information on this phenomena.

One of the five tribes Kotkin focuses on is *India.* As with many ethnic groups, we sometimes associate Indians with their restaurants. However, their neighbors, the Pakistanis, seem to have their niche in the hotel/motel business. The co-author of the book you are reading (Charlie Dygert) has been in contact and working with various Indian entrepreneurs in the fields of steel making, foundries, and software. Their migration and dispersion, as Kotkin refers to it, is expanding to many countries and many fields. Kotkin explores why each particular group is so able to do this.

In the case of India, we believe this has been accelerated by the fact that the bureaucracy in their homeland is so burdensome that it is much easier to cast one's economic lot on other waters. In time, when the government is finally able to become more streamlined, the Indians, who have made their wealth and learned their trade abroad, will return and build up the same industries in their homeland. The current loser in all of this is India itself, whose own policies keep it in a rather backward state of affairs.

The manager, practicing in the global marketplace needs to know, first, that this phenomena (which has happened down through history) is continuing and who the main groups involved are. Second, they need to learn how to work effectively with these dispersed groups of people.

GROUP DYNAMICS

A special field of study that has its roots in both psychology and sociology is called "Group Dynamics." It is founded on the work of Wilhelm Wundt (1821-1920) and has become a major force in management research and application.

Two of the early pioneers of this theory developed guidelines on how to most effectively work in groups

—particularly "work groups." They are:

Wilfred Bion (1897-1979)

This influential Englishman became president of the British Psychoanalytical Society. Working with military units, he began to notice certain behaviors among the various groups.

In his notable book, *Experience in Groups,* Bion presented his two major management theories.

Theory 1:"Theory of the Herd." He contended that all people are social (or pack) animals—and group oriented. In addition, he proposed that individual action is a myth and there is only group action. So as leaders we are to maximize this connection.

Theory 2: "Work vs Non-Work." The "work group" is concerned with the basic task at hand. The "non-work group," behaves as though certain assumptions are held by those in this category (that the group is either dependent on a strong leader, needs to protect itself, or need each other for survival).

Kurt Lewin (1890-1947)

It was Lewin who coined the term "Group Dynamics" —describing the positive and negative forces within groups of people. He was focused on how this study could be applied to social issues in the real world.

Lewin was born in Prussia and did his early research in Germany. In 1940, he emigrated to the United States, and eventually taught at Stanford, Cornell, and MIT. His book,

Revolving Social Conflicts, is considered a classic.

He held that "All actions are based on the ground a person happens to stand on. The firmness; of their actions and clearness of their decisions depend largely upon the stability of that ground. Whatever a person does or wishes to do, they must have some ground to stand on."

He defines a team as a collection of people with a shared, common fate. So, if you desire a high-performing team, make it clearly understood that whatever happens to one happens to all.

THE INNER CIRCLE

In the workplace, we need to grasp the importance of how sociology works in the day-to-day operation of our enterprise or association, profit or non-profit.

Whether formal or informal, each organization has a leader—and each has an inner circle. It is through this inner circle that ideas are created, discussed, and moved to the "outer circle," or general enterprise. These are circles of influence.

Who is in the inner circle? And who is not? The formal structure of an organization chart is not often the "directory" where we find out who these people are. We must dig deeper.

In the inner circle, trust, personal loyalty, communication, and willingness to spread the leader's agenda are strong ingredients for membership. In turn, if these unwritten covenants are not broken, the members of the inner circle may stay shielded from [organizational] harm—as long as the current leader remains in power.

This special circle is very instrumental in how the organization survives, grows, develops, and forms its culture. If the mission of the members is to be support-based and merely helps carry out the tasks as assigned by the leader, physical talents may be the ones required.

However, in our competitive world of business, education, medicine, etc., many leaders are more interested in building a team who can help them deal with current complexities. If this is the issue, how can we measure one's ability to deal with it? If we want a high performance team, based on a scale of "10", do we want all 10's?

An inner circle can be an asset when its purpose is to support the mission of the organization and help drive its vision. But if it has a different agenda, conflict results. When the CEO has an inner circle with an unstated game plan that opposes the company's mission—it turns toxic!

A TEAM OF RIVALS

The question always comes up: "What's the best way to select a management team?" Well, in our experience, there is no perfect way, since the dynamic among all people is complex—and all teams develop some negative habits.

However, it is worth noting how Abraham Lincoln

decided to form his Cabinet after being named President. The process is described in the book by Doris Kearns Goodwin, *A Team of Rivals.* She writes that Lincoln's "unprecedented decision to incorporate his eminent rivals into his political family, the cabinet, was evidence of a profound self-confidence and a first indication of what would prove to others a most unexpected greatness."

The fact was that every member he chose for his administration was better known, better educated, more experienced than Lincoln, Most would have seen that as threatening. But, as Goodwin details, "It soon became clear, however, that Abraham Lincoln would emerge the undisputed captain of this most unusual cabinet, truly a team of rivals. The powerful competitors who had originally disdained Lincoln became colleagues who helped him steer the country through its darkest days."

"TEAM BALL"

If you recall watching the 2014 NBA playoffs between the San Antonio Spurs and the Miami Heat, it was like a modern story of Sociology and Anthropology played out in real time. Most people thought Miami, with their superstar, Lebron James, would dominate, but they failed to understand the dynamic that Greg Popovich, long-time coach of the Spurs, brought to the series.

San Antonio had players from the far corners of the world: Italy, Virgin Islands, Brazil, Argentina,, two from France, two from Australia—as well as those born in the U.S. How did he mold them into such a highly successful unit?

Popovich used a total team approach. When they were on the road, the Spurs ate all their meals together. On the court, it was "team ball." Since they all could shoot well, they kept passing the ball around until someone had an open shot. Observers called it "shared fate" in action.

Yes, Tim Duncan had plenty of leadership, but under Popovich, the team was more important than any individual. Said the coach, "We're not an athletic team. We don't jump over people and do 360s. What we have is our smarts and our system."

That's how the Spurs won the series!

THE AGENDA

Every organization, regardless of size, should have an agenda—a list of things to be done or dealt with. It reveals the story of what the enterprise plans to do, or not do. The "time frame" or scope of the agenda may be measured in minutes or in decades. In the process, as each new day dawns, the question on the table is: *what is on our docket today?* However, there are two additional questions that are equally as important: (1) Who decides what the agenda is? (2) How is this process carried out?

In reality, each person in the organization comes to work carrying his or her agenda with them. These individual priorities may be in concert with the company's mission, or they may not be. So the question each day is the same: what is the game plan? It may shift from time to time.

Some may ask, "So what?" What difference does it make what each person's individual agenda is? Isn't it true that every team member knows what their job is and what is expected of them? Unfortunately it is not so simple.

Many organizations formalize the agenda in a number of ways:

- Mission statement
- Statement of purpose
- Goals
- Objectives
- Charter
- Policies and procedures
- Standards
- Strategic plan

Does everyone in the organization know what each of these are? Are they privy to seeing them? Will everyone interpret each of these written documents in the same way?

Daily, every individual arrives with:

- His/her agenda
- His/her "bag of energy"
- His/her sense of purpose or lack of purpose
- An attitude: good or bad
- Passion, or lack thereof

- Humility or arrogance
- Encouragement or ego
- Being ready to contribute or a heart full of mischief

We see how they are dressed, what they are carrying in their hands, whether they are smiling or not, and many other evident factors; but how do we find where they stand in regard to the list above?

This is when we start the process, or in some cases actually trigger the fuse, by what we call "The Encounter Rule." This is the first contact between a member in the organization and someone they are working for or with [i.e., the person they report to]. If this tends to go badly, day after day, then other negative things follow.

In almost every case, this all takes place before any actual *work* is started. The damage done by this time can assure us that very little, if any, constructive output will be accomplished at all.

But what would be the outcome if everyone came in with a single-minded purpose of passionately carrying out the organization's mission by *together* working on the agenda for that day? Well, for one thing, performance would improve. This could result in a self-directed work team where very little management is required.

THE "MULTIPLE AGENDA" PROBLEM

The higher up the ladder the "multiple" agenda problem

exists, the more serious it will be. It is far too common to find that the *chosen few* at the top of the pyramid, who have been given the responsibility to direct and lead, each have their own plan and timetable.

Why would these special people have an agenda other than the company's? In most cases they are driven by one or more of these factors:

- Power
- Recognition
- Control
- Getting even
- Personal wealth [gain]
- Insecurity
- Paranoia
- Fear
- Fairness [or lack thereof]

I am sure that other items could be added to the list. It is the human or personality traits that each of us possess which determine what our plan may be.

Our personal agenda is driven and created by what motivates us. If we have no self-motivation, our objective is probably to do as little as possible. Occasionally, every one of us experiences a bad day—and our goal is just to make it to the closing hour and head for home.

Over time, our individual agenda is driven by our beliefs

and values, which then influence our behavior. If our purpose is in concert with the organization's, there is a high probability that our management or "work style" is compatible with the culture of the enterprise.

If we come with a good attitude, plenty of energy and passion, and with the right skill sets, we then have a strong chance of being a high performer.

Here's the best part; high performers tend to migrate to others like them, and before long we are seeing fantastic results.

On the flip side of that coin, when our personal agenda is not synchronized with the company's, we will most likely develop "an attitude." This means we have chosen to move from being part of the solution to becoming part of the problem. The following behaviors surface:

- Victim thinking
- "Get even" behavior
- Negative attitudes
- Pessimistic thinking—all the time

If an organization does not have an agenda [hopefully in the form of a *living* strategic plan] then each day it drifts with the winds of need as tasks are performed to take care of the problems of the moment. "Fire fighters" emerge—as people get a lot of practice—and this soon becomes the organization's *norm.*

- The squeaky wheel gets the grease
- The paper on top of the stack gets action
- The latest phone call, e-mail, or text message drives the current activity
- We have a high proficiency for knowing how to blame others
- We rarely trust anyone, including ourselves, because we "don't know"

An organization operating in this chaotic state of equilibrium will continue to survive as long as there is "just enough":

- Just enough money to make payroll
- Just enough orders to stay busy
- Just enough receivables to gain credit
- Just enough stretch of payables to squeak by another day
- Just enough people to get orders out the door
- Just enough space
    – And the list goes on.

With no game plan, and no time to worry about one, each person in the organization simply becomes a task-oriented worker. The objective is to show up and "move the freight" each day, every day. As long as nothing upsets the apple cart, it will somehow survive. But if a major change occurs, there is no mechanism in place to give notice, so at some point, the organization will just crash. Surprise, surprise!

AN EXCITING STORY TO TELL

When there is an agenda, this creates something that everyone can have an opinion on. It is also where strong, confident, convincing leadership must be present. The blueprint, which is now in the outline of a strategic plan, should be put into word pictures in the form of a story—"our story."

The leader must tell the story to everyone in the organization—not once, but repeatedly. Since each member of the team will interpret this in his/her own way; the leader must be adept at painting the picture in a manner that everyone can understand.

Next, it is essential that every person in the organization learn the narrative and begin to tell it over and over. The agenda becomes the story; the story becomes the agenda. Everyone must personalize and internalize it—taking owner-ship.

When this happens, it becomes part of the culture—and it shapes the history of the company. Beliefs and values are suddenly real and behavior is more predictable. The drama shifts to accounts of success in carrying out the mission. Many organizations have done this successfully for a time—but most have not, and don't even have a clue!

Stuck-in-the-mud enterprises start to use the phrase: "This

is our tradition." However "stuff happens," and transformation is required. But now our old agenda, which has become our culture and developed our tradition, is faced with a new opponent—change. It is time for a new game plan. So what do we need to do?

Now we begin to see the picture of why we need astute and aware people in management and leadership. We always need to be looking for ways to improve, change, grow, and develop—and this involves choices. These choices will strongly influence what the new agenda will become.

To make some sense of all of this, we begin to build "change processes." For example, a yearly review of our strategic direction [plan] is such a process.

Where do we start?

We must first look at where we are. "How are we doing?" The management gurus and university professors have blessed us with a wide assortment of tools. Software developers have taken these tools and now offer a variety of computer-related formats to help us find the answer to problems of all sorts.

DESIGNING THE NEW GAME PLAN

We investigate our magical tool kit and select a "SWOT analysis." What is this? We ask selected individuals to list, in their opinion, our organization's:

40

- Strengths
- Weaknesses
- Opportunities
- Threats

We take the same group and "brainstorm"— opening the discussion just like we would open up Pandora's box. "Let's begin to make a list of all the problems we currently are facing." We take the list and organize it into categories; then we examine and compare our data.

Guess what? From this, we begin to itemize "things we need to do"—developing priorities and calling them goals. We create and assign ways of measuring our results.

In this process we build a new agenda. Then comes the most exciting part of all: we begin to tell the new story.

This is sociology in action!

Notes for the Playbook

- Sociology involves group dynamics.
- Narcissistic leaders and managers are headed for failure.
- Our global economy requires that we master the art of working with diverse cultures.
- The "inner circle" of an enterprise must totally support its mission.

- Every employee must embrace the organization's agenda, not their own.
- Alignment within the management team is vital.
- The strategic plan must become the "story" of an enterprise.
- We design a new game plan by a SWOT analysis —looking at Strengths, Weaknesses, Opportunities, and Threats.
- Change comes by establishing priorities, setting goals, and developing ways to measure progress.

DISCIPLINE #3

PHILOSOPHY

*I have a new philosophy. I'm
only going to dread one day at a time.*
– Charles M. Schulz

A frustrated young man was complaining to his minister that he didn't like his new job; it didn't seem to hold much of a future for him. The clergyman asked him to elaborate.

"Well, here's the way it works," the fellow began. "Each newly hired person receives 100 points, but each time you mess up or fail, one point is subtracted. And in the case of a major 'screw-up' two points are deducted. When you fall down to 80 points, you are expected to pack up your stuff and leave."

"But," the minister asked, "isn't there any way to add points when you do something well?"

"No," the young man replied, "with this boss, there is no way you can increase your number."

How would you like to work for a leader or manager who was always looking for the negative, never the positive?

A belief that people are basically good can result in a feeling that employees will normally be productive when provided with the right tools and a healthy environment. However, believing that men and women are fundamentally bad, lazy, dishonest, and unmotivated will generate an entirely different approach to leadership and management.

The facts bear out that the most prevalent management style continues to be authoritarian, based on the underlying notion that people cannot be trusted on their own. However, we are now finding out that, in many cases, self-directing work teams not only can be trusted, they may not require any direct supervision at all. Could the managers be the problem?

LOOKING INSIDE

The feeling or belief you have about people will form the keystone for your *personal management philosophy.* This implies that all who are or wish to be in a leadership role must take this first dramatic fork in the road which will categorize us in one of two "populations" from this point forward.

To build a manager we need to look inside the individual to discover both the "talk" and the "walk" regarding:

- Values
- Beliefs
- Attitudes
- Behaviors
- Skills

The order is important. The list may have additions, but no deletions. In other words, you can climb from 80 back to 100!

To see how you stack up, make an outline of what your values are so you can look at what you have written and ask, "Is this what I *truly* believe in?" If it isn't, take a pen and strike it out.

The categories you select to be in *your personal management philosophy* may differ from ours, however, there are certain ones that just can't be ignored.

Here is how your list might look:

- People Policy—being concerned with people as individuals, not with who is right.
- Relationships between leadership, management, and "the rest of the employees."
- Communication—soliciting opinions, listening, showing respect.
- Work Ethic—responsibility, accountability, making a contribution to the company.
- Performance—using good judgment, raising the bar, improving quality.
- Values—practicing high ethics and setting an example of what is right.
- Time Management—making minutes count.
- Leadership—demonstrating intelligence, stability, empathy, social sensitivity, moral courage, resilience.

- Business Knowledge/Philosophy—mastering the economics of your enterprise. Becoming a systems thinker.
- Customers—understanding their importance to our future.
- Culture—building a positive team chemistry and a total environment for success.
- Management Style—being enthusiastic about getting to work and making things happen. Always seeing the big picture.

This list is further detailed in our book, *Managing for Success.*

Another equally valid approach would be to combine personal values and the "expectations" of the organization's stakeholders. Such a list might look like this:

- Personal values and ethics
- Management Style
- Communications
- Customers
- Employees
- Stockholders
- Suppliers
- Debt Holders
- Stock Analysts
- Government
- Community

The development and occasional review and revision of your management and leadership philosophy is crucial. It is your list, but it should be reviewed with your mentor(s) or trusted associates. However, you may not want to share it 100% with everyone. Why? Because they have their own philosophy, which is likely different than yours. There is no right or wrong, but a continual striving to find "what works best for you."

If you choose not to bother with having such a philosophy, chances are you will not have a *conscious* management style. But remember this, a leader with "no style" is like a chameleon—changing with the surroundings. The person may survive as an employee but will gain little respect as a manager.

Your personal philosophy of leadership, the inner thoughts and beliefs which you internalize, become the "function" that consumes your thinking and is a mental shadow during most of your waking hours. For some, it spins in their head, even when they are trying to rest.

These thoughts develop over time based on events, experience, and the gaining of knowledge. You find yourself constantly building and analyzing different mental models of a situation. The dilemma: which to choose; how will you know; what do you do if you pick a poor one?

Your management style becomes your "delivery and receiving" system as you go about your daily duties. With this philosophy imbedded in your brain like bedrock, you start to experience the activities of the day. How you go about inter-acting with these events says volumes about your style.

FLOW OR DISCORD?

The impact of your style can be summed up as either flow or discord. The same individual may use both, depending on the situation, however, most will follow one or the other. Either you try to remove barriers to keep the company running smoothly toward its goals or you intervene to redirect employees. The first is cooperative in nature, the latter is disruptive.

Generally, a leader who seeks the course of *flow* will, over time, achieve better cooperation and results from the individuals being directed. This is because such an approach drives out fear and helps the enterprise concentrate on the customer. On the other hand, discord steers the focus back on the boss and redirects energy to please him or her.

A management outlook will determine how you approach situations and implement leadership. It may be based on observations, practical experience, extensive reading, or example from a mentor or teacher.

GET READY FOR CHANGE

To many, it seems, management is a series of functions that are accomplished by use of defined tools and techniques in a very finite toolkit. This approach is not unlike a skilled carpenter who is called upon to make "quantum" (e.g., like in 'big') repairs to an old house. The carpenter comes in with his notepad and takes a walk-around. Two days later he/she submits an estimate of cost to the owner who gives it a thumbs up or a thumbs down. With a thumbs up; the next question is: "When can you start?" The answer: "Immediately."

With this settled, the carpenter retrieves his tools from his truck and begins. Six months later the house looks as good as new.

The reason this approach is hard to duplicate in the workplace is because a leader is not a carpenter. You see, the carpenter, for the most part, could rely on finding the work he had finished the previous day still in place when he returned the next morning. He soon learns to depend upon this, day after day, until the very end of the project. The exceptions, if caused by external human intervention, could be solved by locking the door each day as he left, or if by natural causes (e.g. rain), could be avoided by "covering up."

Some managers and leaders mistakenly feel that by being the last one out and locking up each night, conditions in the morning will be the same as when they left the night before. There is one problem with this: houses do not think; but sometimes people do! The events of yesterday often unravel today.

For those of us who have worked as supervisors, managers, and leaders in continuous-process (24/7) industries, we soon learned to condition ourselves to the reality that nothing stays the same.

It is the conceptual ability to accept this ever-changing reality that helps us make our "second cut."

What do we mean by this?

In "our world," those individuals who cannot honestly say that they feel people are basically *good,* should not move forward in a career as a manager (e.g. first cut). Our second cut is that men and women who are good with *things* but not with people should avoid becoming a manager or leader.

In both of these concept evaluations, we find that *people* is the standard that must be addressed.

MENTAL WORKOUTS!

In terms of philosophy, leaders are credited with the ability to think! Often this is being too kind. It is in this discipline that we provide the opportunity for our mind to truly engage in challenging mental workouts. The difference, of course, between the philosopher and the leader is that the former can continue to spend his/her whole life in the workout room [i.e. the university]; in contrast the "boss" must get out and play the game in the arena where the score is kept and few captives are taken alive. Values, ethics, etc., must become part of oneselves and taken seriously or those in charge will be just a cosmetic shell of a messenger for those surrounding him/her.

Perhaps the early philosophical debates, which did not

lead to conclusions, just more arguments and theories, are the ancestors of the meetings that now consume so much of a leader's time. Many concepts are raised but very few decisions are made.

This makes one ask: *Is the origin of ideas and creativity normally the product of an individual, a group, or a combination?* We ask this because, even though meetings may generate ideas and concepts, they usually conclude without many new ideas. Remember, concentration and commitment are a large part of creativity. Isn't it easier to get these from an individual than from an entire group?

WHAT ARE YOU READING?

Here's an observation that cannot be overlooked. Those climbing the corporate ladder become so engulfed by the tidal waves of business competition, internal crises, and people problems, that they rarely take time to "read" psychology, philosophy, or the other eight essential disciplines that are the focus of this book.

Since balance is needed in everyone's life, it is vital for leaders to carve out time for personal reflection and thinking.

Nothing would please us more than to hear how your thoughts have sprung to life by making the decision to delve into the writings of the great philosophers of history. Here's a short list: Aristotle, Epictetus, Aquinas, Hobbes, Montaigne, Spinoza, Locke, Kant, Hegel, and Mill.

In a nutshell, let us share a small preview of how you will grow:

- Aristotle will sharpen your logic and reasoning.
- Epictetus will teach you that philosophy is a way of life, not just an academic discipline.
- Thomas Aquinas will help you tie theology to great ideas.
- Thomas Hobbes will inspire you to grasp political philosophy.
- Michel de Montaigne will motivate you to apply philosophy to daily living.
- Baruch Spinoza will challenge you to examine your ethics.
- John Locke will help you have a better understanding of identity and self.
- Immanuel Kant will guide you in the linking of reasoning and morality.
- Georg Wilhelm Friedrich Hegel will encourage you to turn contradictions into unity.
- John Stuart Mill will help you understand that self-improvement is the source of true freedom.

LOOKING EAST

It is only natural for Western cultures to turn to Western philosophers for wisdom, starting with Socrates, Plato, and Aristotle. But we can't overlook the influence of the noted thinkers of Asia and the Schools of Classical Chinese Thought, including:

Confucianism:

Confucius (551-479 BC) shared a belief in a heaven that guided all matters in the cosmos and that men were most happy when they were ruled in accordance with the Way (dao). To live a moral, virtuous life was to exist in harmony with the dao. Rites (li) were manifestations of proper conduct, which required wisdom gained through rigorous study, which all were capable of acquiring, by learning from the sage kings, and through the lessons of history.

He believed that all humankind and society itself was perfectible. Each of the five human relationships: father-son, ruler-subject, brother-brother, husband-wife, and friend-friend are nurtured by a distinct virtue and all bonds reciprocal. The Way was the correct socio-moral manner in which human life and politics need be conducted and the superior person (junzi) lived in full accord with it.

Mohism

Mozi (470-391 BC) taught in a manner that was extremely logical, systematic, and utilitarian. He supported maximizing whatever helped people, made their lives better, and increased the peace. Anything that worked against this he deemed gibberish. Mozi believed in an authoritarian social organization with obedience to heaven in almost a religious sense. He vilified the human relationships prized by the Confucians, because they only separated people. Instead he called for "universal love (jian'ai) in which all were respected without reference to family. He despised war so much that he trained his followers in defensive strategies and put them at the service of beleaguered states.

Daoism

In general, Daoism was a philosophy that rejected the organized political and social institutions. Yang Zhu (440–360 BC), who influenced this train of thought, preached the principle of "Each for himself." He was condemned for pure hedonism and self-centeredness, and for showing no concern for the world. He is considered a predecessor of the major Daoist thinkers.

Legalism

This doctrine was spread by Han Fei (280-233 BC). Legalism taught rule by law, not the moral suasion of Confucianism or the anti-authoritarianism of Daoism. It was concerned with how to make the state prosper and continue expanding until the realm was unified. It was a mixture of extreme rationalism, anti-humanitarianism, and totalitarianism. Some Legalists stressed administrative bureaucracy, others strict laws.

Han Fei believed that power was far more important than morality, virtue, or talent. A ruler can be brilliant, he claimed, but without authoritarian powers, nothing will ever be accomplished. He placed no trust in government or society as such, only in laws, for no one could be trusted. He sought rule by strict edicts, with harsh punishment for dissent, but great rewards for service to the ruler.

Sun Tzu

This legendary historical figure (544-496 BC) was a Chinese military general, strategist, and philosopher, who is the author of *The Art of War*—a book that has been read by millions.

He devised strategies for war and the political organizations needed to support it, and also discussed such topics as topography, psychology, and the exploitation of human weaknesses in battle. He was especially attentive to deception and how to use minimal conflict to attain victory. His work extremely influenced 20th century theorists of guerilla warfare. Today, *The Art of War* continues to impact competitive endeavors in culture, politics, sports, and business.

THE SPIRIT OF PHILOSOPHY

In the academic world, philosophy embodies the love of wisdom, which leads to inquiry into principles of reality—or some branch of it including human values or knowledge. In business it becomes our belief system and approach to things.

In today's culture, some in the corporate world have tried to stay away from the very discussion of philosophy because of its historical ties to religion. This issue was discussed by Peter Vaill in his book, *Managing as a Performing Art*, when he observed, "A real premise here is that our tendency to equate discussions of spirit with discussions of religion is a significant part of our problem as a society and as a profession of management and management teachers and consultants. Religion has rendered the question of spirituality almost un-discussible except within a frame of doctrine and language that sound stilted and artificial to many in the world of work. For many of us, spirit is at best discussible only with great self-consciousness and diffidence, and that is a great tragedy. 'Spirituality' for me is the search for a deeper experience of the spirit of various kinds that one can feel stirring within."

In truth, morals and management cannot be separated. Leaders represent the company in action. If they are dishonest or corrupt, as some are, the company and many of those associated with it will also be tarnished. The effect of breaching contracts and agreements is demoralizing: "If I can't trust you once, I will probably never trust you again."

Reputations are extremely difficult to rebuild.

OUR SURVIVAL IS AT STAKE

We need to take seriously the words of Ken Blanchard and Michael O'Connor in their notable book, *Managing by Values.* They write, "Perhaps more than at any previous time, an organization today must know what it stands for and on what principles it will operate. No longer is values-based organizational behavior an interesting philosophical choice—it is a requisite for survival."

And they add, "The particular mix of dilemmas in which

competitive companies do business nowadays requires that they build success upon effectiveness. Once an organization has a clear picture of its mission and values, it has a strong basis for evaluating its management practices and bringing them into alignment with the articulated mission and values."

What about you? How much time have you given to developing a personal leadership philosophy? Has it been formulated clearly? Can you articulate this? Can you teach it to someone else?

Notes for your Playbook

- Decide what you truly believe about people.
- Be able to articulate your personal management or leadership philosophy.
- Analyze whether your style results in cooperation or disruption.
- Carve out time for personal reflection and thinking.
- Read the writings of the great Eastern and Western philosophers.
- Seek ways to apply time-tested wisdom to your daily work.
- Do not be afraid of the spiritual aspect of leadership.
- Make it your objective to teach your leadership philosophy to others.

DISCIPLINE #4

GEOGRAPHY

Don't overlook the importance of worldwide thinking. A company that keeps its eye on Tom, Dick, and Harry is going to miss Pierre, Hans, and Yoshio.
– Al Ries

Following World War II, companies were still not permitted to build new industrial plants on "green grass" sites. However, it was permissible to convert an old facility into a new one. Such was the case with two plants Brockway Glass owned in Oklahoma.

I (Richard Jacobs writing) recall that the first, was in 1945 when my father (a career executive with Brockway) moved to Muskogee, with our family, to convert an old glass casket factory into a *modern* glass container plant. The two other company-owned factories at that time were both located in the small western Pennsylvania town of Brockway, which was "cool" nearly all year around because of the altitude of the adjacent hills.

By comparison, the long Oklahoma summers were oppressively hot. These were the days prior to the use of air conditioning. Window fans and swimming pools were the height of comfort.

Finley Hess, was an executive vice-president at the time, the person to whom my dad reported. Finley was very intelligent and knew the glass business, but also liked his *creature comforts*. It was bad enough being a scotch drinker visiting in what was then a "dry state," but having to endure the heat too!

One day, he just couldn't stand it anymore and blurted out: "We've got to be crazy to come to the hottest place on earth and build a huge fire!" He was referring to the glass furnace which had internal temperatures approaching 3000 degrees Fahrenheit.

Over the next 42 two years, Brockway Glass continued to grow, become an industry leader and a billion dollar company. In 1987 the firm was sold to Owens-Illinois Inc., in Toledo, Ohio (my home town). Many of the original plants remain in production and have become part of the world's largest glass container manufacturer.

From earliest times, archaeologists have studied clay pots, ceramics, and earthen vessels to learn about ancient civilizations. Clear, pristine glass has provided the containers for canned foods, sealed baby food, liquids of all sorts, and multiple uses for the benefit of society. Glass containers are one of the often over looked but vital industries for all civilizations.

So, the company didn't just expand to Oklahoma, but now has thriving plants in Europe, Asia, and Latin America.

A WORLDWIDE STAGE

As we examine the discipline of GEOGRAPHY, it has two major aspects in the business world. First, it impacts the globalization of manufacturing and services. Second, it applies to the physical layout of a particular office or location. At the end of this chapter, we will discuss a third aspect: the importance of having a working knowledge of geography itself. Let's begin with the international considerations.

In the second act of *As You Like It,* the famous play written in the early 1600s by William Shakespeare, he penned these words: "All the world's a stage. And all the men and woman merely players."

If Shakespeare could have looked ahead a half a millennium he would have seen men and women literally playing their roles on an instant global platform through digital communications, air transportation, and multinational corporations.

A SHRINKING PLANET

Companies that were founded in the United States now have their footprints, factories, and facilities in the nations of the world—giants such as General Motors, ExxonMobile, McDonald's, and General Electric.

We no longer are surprised to see a journalist standing on the main street of some remote town in China or the Congo with Colonel Sanders smiling on a sign of a Kentucky Fried

Chicken store in the background.

International commerce has become so commonplace, that some of the largest corporations in America are now owned by foreign interests. For example:

- Anheuser-Bush Brewery was founded in St. Louis, but is now owned by InBev, with headquarters located in Belgium.
- Virginia based pork producer, Smithfield, was recently purchased by a Chinese holding company.
- Vaseline was created in Brooklyn, NY, and became a valued U.S. company until it was bought by the UK-Dutch conglomerate, Unilever.
- Purina was started in Missouri by William H. Danforth, but is now part of the Swiss company, Nestle.
- 7-Eleven began in Dallas and grew to more than 50,000 units. It is now owned by a Japanese holding company.

It comes as a surprise to many Americans that companies they assume to be born and bred in the good old USA are actually imports.

- When you pull into a BP gas station, you may have seen enough of their commercials to think it stands for "Better Products," but it's actually UK-owned British Petroleum.

- Bayer Aspirin came to the United States from Germany.
- You'll find a box of plastic Lego bricks in the closet of practically every American kid, but the company was founded by Ole Kirk Christiansen in Denmark—and still has its headquarters there.

Issues of Expansion

The lure of globalization is hard to resist, yet, as business leaders, we need to be aware of what we may be facing.

Let's say you started a sandwich shop in Dallas that specialized in a variety of sandwiches that were low calorie and had healthy ingredients. But people started beating a path to your door because of the special sauce you created with "secret ingredients."

Word of mouth was so good that you opened a second store across town and called both locations, "Sam's Savory Sandwiches"—or some other name you could trademark.

Soon, customer's were coming in, asking, "Why can't we have one of these in Oklahoma City?" Well, economics dictate that there's no way to find the up-front money to start building new stores before your initial investment turns a substantial profit. So you decide to franchise, perhaps charging an initial license fee (for a specific geographical territory), creating a training program, requiring certain policies and procedures, and receiving a small percent of the gross (not the profits, because you may never see any) of the new store.

Suddenly, you are faced with a fresh reality. How can you sell a franchise in another state without hiring a lawyer in that state to file the Offering Circular, disclosure statement required by the FTC, and pay the fees required by the Attorney General's office of that state? You just don't announce, "I'm going to franchise." Yet, despite the hurdles, you decide to expand.

Then someone walks in from Madrid, Manila, or Mumbai and says, "This would be a big hit in my country. Can I start one of these back home?"

The very thought of a huge international operation makes you think you've just won the lottery. But before you become a global enterprise, you'd better spend time finding the answers to some vital questions:

- What legal system do they have?
- How stable is the government?
- What are the economic policies regarding foreign-held businesses?
- Are the accounting standards different than ours?
- How big will the language barriers be?
- What about currency exchange rates?
- Will I have to pay taxes in both the foreign country and the US?
- Will there be tariffs on the "special sauce" I send over, or will I have to disclose my secret recipe?
- What do I need to know about the corporate culture?

—and there will probably be a hundred other factors that crop up.

It may be wise to think of foreign expansion in terms of risks. What are the financial risks? What are the terrorism risks? Etc.

As a side note, you have to be very careful of language issues when naming your products. For example, a widely-marketed candy bar in Poland is named "Fart" (it translates as "lucky bar"). In Iran, they sell a detergent called "Barf!" And visitors to Ghana are shocked to look on the grocery shelves and see an extremely popular soda, "Pee Cola."

"LOCATION, LOCATION, LOCATION"

Closer to home, geography plays a far larger role in the success of a business than most imagine. Oh, it's nice to say, "If we build it, they will come,"—but those stories are few and far between. This is why companies pay top dollar to consultants who research a community's traffic patterns, income stratification, and dozens of other factors before making a bid to buy a piece of property or lease a building for their expansion.

In business, you often hear the phrase, "It's price, price, price." But to those who know best, "It's location, location, location."

More and more, the experts are turning to computerized mapping that shows amazing detail of a particular area. Today, you can type in a location on Google and take a virtual tour, following the arrows up and down streets, looking at the buildings, and examining the neighborhood as if you were actually there.

With a little more research you can utilize economic geography and location theory (business zoning, tax break areas, etc.).

Then we can turn to population and settlement studies (including crime reports on specific communities).

Another factor that leaders and managers need to know is how geography impacts corporate culture. For instance, traditional dress codes may be found in an employee policy manual for a New York office. But if you look at the company's rules for their Los Angeles branch, the dress requirements may be much more casual

Is this because of the weather? Local social attitudes? Or what? We have been asked, "Why do some leaders succeed so well in one place and not another? Is it the "people," the "culture," the "situation?"—or just pure luck? In our observations, leaders who are strong on vision, mission, and commitment, but flexible creating an enjoyable work atmosphere seem to do best.

THE WORKING ENVIRONMENT

In looking at geography, we cannot overlook the physical layout of your office, whether it is a small operation or one with hundreds of employees.

There are two major opinions on how the working environment should be created.

One: A closed concept, where each worker has his or her own cubicle, and separate areas where teams meet from time to time.

Two: An open office, with hardly any barriers; where every employee can be seen by their associates.

We wish we could tell you that there are only two opinions on the topic, but that's hardly the case. Those who like the "open" concept say:

- "It makes it so much easier to interact with others."
- "I think it generates a sense of camaraderie."
- "The flow of information is much faster."
- "I like asking someone for advice without knocking on their door."

The "bean counters" like the open floor plan because it cuts down on construction costs, lighting expenses, and improves air flow. Plus, adding space for new staff can be much easier.

But before making a decision on the use of space, we have to listen to the dissenters:

- "I hate it. There is far too much noise and I can't concentrate on my work."
- "The distractions are so many that I don't feel as productive."
- "The lack of privacy really hampers my use of the phone—even when I'm talking to a client."

- "If I come to work with a cold, I feel like I'm spreading it to the whole staff."
- "I could adjust the lighting and heat in my former office, now I can't."

You may ask, "Okay Jacobs and Dygert. What do you recommend?"

Since we've seen open offices succeed and fail, you should assign a task force that spends time with every employee before recommending or embarking on change. In general, young employees who know how to multi-task, thrive in an open atmosphere. Older employees who like to focus on a specific assignments aren't so keen.

Most important, if you put your stamp of approval on a major change in the office geography and it doesn't work, you will be applauded for admitting your error and moving to another floor plan. You'll receive five stars for flexibility!

AN OPEN DOOR POLICY?

While we are on the topic of the office layout, as a leader or manager, you need to make a decision on whether to personally have an open door policy—or not.

There are some real "pluses" to such a move:

- It is a sign that you're accessible.
- It encourages openness and transparency.

- It gives employees the feeling that they can share problems and address issues whenever the need arises.
- It fosters an environment of mutual respect.
- It signals that you welcome collaboration.
- It lets leadership keep a pulse on what is happening in the company.

But what are the "minuses"?

- Some employees fear speaking openly to management, afraid they will be criticized as a troublemaker.
- If a lower-level employee goes "straight to the top," middle management may think they are being bypassed, and tensions can arise.
- Your work may be interrupted so often that you have a hard time finishing projects.
- Your confidential phone conversations may be overheard.
- Certain employees may infringe on your time far too often.

Some leaders have solved part of the problem by creating a schedule which lets the staff know that the door is open just certain hours each work day.

All things being equal, you'll be given more thumbs up than thumbs down if your door is left open.

UNDERSTANDING THE DISCIPLINE

We have been looking at geography as it relates to multinational corporations, business locations, and the physical layout of the office. However, there are many advantages to having an understanding of the discipline of geography itself.

When you start putting the pieces together, you'll see how this knowledge will help you develop the "big picture" of our world—and how it affects your business and leadership.

In addition you will grasp how geography has a tremendous influence on all other disciplines due to:

- Size (of a nation, region, or city)
- Weather (favorable or unfavorable to crops and man)
- Natural resources (for development, industrialization, growth)
- Location (how far, from what else)
- Accessability (or the lack of it)
- Natural terrain (rivers, lakes, mountains, shoreline, crop-growing land, swamps, jungles, etc.)
- Animals who habitat there
- Culture (friendliness of the people)

In one way or another, all of these can be linked to geography—which looks at the surface of our planet and its physical, economic, biological, political, and demographic characteristics and their interrelationships.

In the words of Norwegian professor and author, Arild

Holt-Jensen, "A cultivation of the powers of observation is ... an important objective in the education of a geographer. It is of primary importance to learn how to 'see geographically' —to observe and interpret a natural or cultural landscape without having to have local knowledge of it. Geographical training develops a distinct method of observation aimed at understanding of the form of culture and landscape in quite a different way from that of the ordinary tourist. The lack of ability to observe in this way distinguishes most travel writers from geographers."

Holt-Jensen has categorized the study of this discipline to include the following:

- Historical geography
- Cultural geography
- Humanistic geography
- Landscape studies
- Computer mapping
- Population and settlement studies
- Economic geography
- Location theory
- Behavioral geography
- Social physics
- Time-space geography
- Human ecology

A NEVER-ENDING QUEST

What events have brought us to this point?

Ancient Greeks, such as Herodotus (485-425 BC) gave topographical descriptions of the known world, and placed historical events in a geographical setting. We also find detailed descriptions of the land and it's impact on peoples and events in the Old and New Testaments of the Bible.

History records the works of noted Islamic geographers of the Middle ages including Ibn Batuta (1304-1368) and Ibn Khaldum (1332-1406). Arab traders traveled widely.

Early explorers enlightened the world, describing and mapping continents. These include Marco Polo (1265), Christopher Columbus (1492) Magellan (1519), Sir Francis Drake (1577). And we should not forget Lewis and Clark exploring America (1804).

Even though Immanuel Kant (1724-1804) was a German philosopher, his research regarding the races of man and their physical activities on earth added a new dimension of geographical studies.

Charles Darwin's 1859 book, *On the Origin of Species,* sparked an interest in human geography—examining the relationship between nature and man (struggle and survival).

As an academic discipline, however, geography came into vogue in the mid-nineteenth century in Germany.

About the same time, there was a rush to establish colonial powers in many distant lands, this led to the early development of international trade and the formation of a long list of geographical societies.

As time progressed, attention has turned to how this discipline interacts with others. For example, in 1919, Nevin M. Fenneman, geology professor at the University of

Wisconsin, described the relationship of geography with six other sciences: geology, meteorology, biology, economics, history, and sociology.

What does the future hold? If the moon landing of Neil Armstrong and the crew of Apollo 11 is any indication, discoveries in outer space tell us that the study of geography has no boundaries.

Notes for your Playbook

- International commerce is a reflection of our shrinking world.
- Before expanding globally, examine the risks.
- Locally, pay close attention to economic and cultural geography.
- Understand the pros and cons regarding the physical layout of your office space.
- Decide whether you will have an "open door" policy.
- Studying geography gives you the "big picture" of our world.
- Know the historical events that have shaped the study of lands, commerce, and human interaction.
- Have an appreciation for how geography is inter-twined with other disciplines.

HISTORY

The danger of the past was that men
became slaves. The danger of the future is
that men may become robots.
– Erich Fromm

If you've never read George Orwell's thought-provoking book, *Animal Farm*, we recommend that you do. At first you may think it's about the dangers of socialism and communism, but it is really a primer on leadership and management.

The manager, "Farmer Jones," was the owner of one of the many farms dotting the countryside of England. As with all the other farmers, Jones decided who would do what work, how much each would get to eat, and he reaped the surplus. He was the only person to live in the comforts of a house, where he consumed as much food and drink as he wished.

Farmer Jones had the choice of education to the extent that he could read from books and gain new insights and knowledge. He had choices for entertainment. He could wander into town with the surplus profits and purchase goods for his further enjoyment. Plus, he had companionship in the form of his wife, Mrs. Jones.

The farm animals were all contributors, giving of their physical efforts day in and day out. They consumed only the food given to them by Jones or from the pasture land in the summer. Their comforts were few; they lived where assigned.

However, this particular group of animals had developed a sort of intelligence, led by the pigs. They created appropriate slogans and guidelines for their plight. Eventually a small revolution occurred and Farmer Jones was driven from his land. His wife also escaped and they took up residence in the town. The animals took charge of the farm—well almost. The pigs grabbed the management duties; but everything stayed pretty much the same for the rest of the animals.

Farmer Jones and several of his neighboring farmers made a couple of unsuccessful attempts at regaining control of his farm, but the animals drove them off. Over time the pigs, who had appointed themselves as the leaders, moved into the farm house and started to delight in the same comforts that Farmer Jones had once enjoyed. They also started to demonstrate the identical behavior pattern of superiority over the rest of the animals. Among the pigs, there were several palace revolts in which power was gained or lost until one pig became supreme. This pig had other pigs as assistants but also guard dogs, trained from pups, to be his own army. In time, the pigs gained knowledge and even negotiated "farm deals" with human neighbors, etc. The plight of the other animals deteriorated from poor to bad.

A windmill was built as a status symbol and a tribute to the planning and cunning of the leaders—the pigs. The guidelines written in the days of the farmer were constantly modified to the benefit of the swine. Slogans were changed; purges were held; animals were killing animals. The pigs were, in time, able to restore all of the dreaded practices without making any permanent corrections for the other animals' welfare.

This might all have been written to foretell the advent of what to expect under communism—and it has turned out to be true. But there is a lesson here for us as well.

When we are unhappy about something at work, we look for someone to blame. In many cases the workers blame the boss. If only that "old SOB" were out of here, everything would be great. But what happens when that despised boss finally retires? Someone takes his place. It is not too long before the "new SOB" is disliked even more. Suddenly there is a yearning for the "good old days."

The lesson is to change the system, change the culture, and take on the responsibility of getting it right.

What do we learn from history? These same communists went to great lengths to rewrite the past in order to put themselves in a much more favorable light—just as George Orwell said they would.

THE WELL-TRAVELED ROAD

Closer to home, what do our own history books tell us about our Native Americans? What is the true story? Why *was* the civil war actually fought? According to some, the reason is now being rewritten or, at least, modified to satisfy a large segment of our population—the African-Americans.

When Henry Ford and others hired workers "from the neck down," was that any different than Farmer Jones and his farm animals? No, they were both being used for their physical efforts. In Farmer Jones' case, the animals were fed just enough so that they could contribute to the work effort day after day. Henry Ford, although he did not seem interested in the worker's minds, was interested in their pocketbooks. He wanted them to be not only workers, but customers. He certainly desired that they have enough money to purchase one of his black machines off the Ford assembly line.

In the business literature, we are reading that in the current century there is an acute need for innovation and anticipation to go along with excellence, productivity, quality, technology, and cost containment. We are being told that the future of the US as a market leader will be directly dependent upon our ability to set things right in our public and private school systems. We are challenged that in the Age of Knowledge, it is what is in the *head* of the workers that will matter most.

Many have concluded that when employees are

contributing with both their physical and mental efforts in an atmosphere of collaboration and cooperation, the need for management, will become less and less. Yet, there will always be a place for a visionary leader.

Will the system change? Farmer Jones was just doing "his thing" like all the other farmers in England. He was not a particularly bad guy, but did gain his livelihood on the backs of his animals. He fed and clothed them adequately and only resorted to "killing" when necessary for food for his table or when the animals' useful days were behind them. He did not engage in political killings.

The pigs came to power on a popular agenda of "freedom to choose" and "more for all." However, very soon, they developed a far meaner system than Farmer Jones had ever thought of.

History tells us that it is the system that must be addressed, not just the personalities. By its very nature, a system is "a bunch of related things." An understanding of this is tough enough, but developing and improving systems is a real chore.

In retrospect, *Animal Farm* is a book on systems development. Since we want to make sure that what we do is for the benefit of all of our stakeholders, the Ten Disciplines will help chart the map to do this.

There are many bumps in the road—but the road has been traveled before.

TELLING THE STORY

As schoolchildren we were often required to memorize dates, names, and places which, for many, made history seem boring. However, history should be the "science of story telling"—made to come alive and be interesting. Children love stories, so do managers. It is our ability to convey the past [and its influence on us today], the present [the account of what is happening now], and the potential impact on the future [often based on what has happened before] that makes history come alive—for countries and for companies. *Tell it in a story, keep it short and interesting, inject humor!*

The narratives of times gone by bring out in vivid detail man's inhumane treatment to each other: The records of wars, occupation of land, theft of property, slavery, ethnic cleansing all show the darker side of mankind. Yet, in all of the stories, the brighter or enlightened side of humanity is told in many accounts of heroic deeds.

The *story of management*, though not as brutal, is often a similar tale. However, as with man himself, it continues to evolve. Modern management in much of its current form has been practiced for about 200 years. However, the story of men directing the lives of others goes back to the beginning of time.

Traditionally, history has been defined as that branch of knowledge concerned with past events, especially those involving human affairs. More specific, it is a record (usually in chronological order) of past events, primarily those concerning a particular field of knowledge, people, or nations.

One of the great purposes served by this discipline is that we are able to see how our present has grown out of yesterday, and is likely to develop in the future.

THE SPIN DOCTORS

One of the dangers of studying history is that much of the "knowledge" comes from the written word, which means that the actual event was interpreted by the author and then reduced to writing and photos. The author's *charge*, purpose, or objectivity can affect *what* is written as much as the event itself. When you study books on American history down through the years, what do they say about the native Americans [e.g. Indians]? A true recording of events as they took place would most likely provide strong reasons for every white person with a European heritage to hang his head in shame.

Have history books been even-handed in their treatment of slavery in America, or for that matter, throughout the world? How many people know that the practice started in Africa by a black brother of the neighboring tribe selling a defeated tribe into bondage? How many can justify the white merchant taking advantage of a political situation for his own economic advantage?

Today, in the world of business, we have to ask: how may

internal reports or even annual reports on companies provide an even-handed account of events? What about the *spin doctors* who take contemporary happenings and report them to someone's best advantage?

AFTER THE BATTLE

There are many lessons and insights that can be gained by a careful study of our great Civil War. Books have been written about Lincoln's abilities in the fields of leadership and management. The debate still rages over whether it was fought over succession from the Union or over slavery. Our history books taught us that it was over succession; but, as we know, these texts become rewritten over time.

We feel that the most amazing aspect of the war was at the very end. Lincoln commanded his generals to return their horses and their guns, and tell the soldiers of the Confederacy to go home and start their lives anew. There were no war recriminations.

Before the war the two sides lived in peace—two different cultures; two different economies. Then, after the battle, peace returned. In the conflict, brother fought brother, but when it was over, the brothers left standing were once again *equals.*

This story should be considered today with the labor issues, strikes, discrimination suits, etc., in our workplace. Solve the problems and move on. No recriminations, but a return to being equals.

SOCIAL HISTORY

As it relates to the Ten Disciplines, we need to investigate what has become known as *social history.* A classic on this subject is *The Age of Enterprise—A Social History of Industrial America,* by Cochran and Miller. Of particular interest is their chapter on "A Philosophy for Industrial Progress," which focuses on the English philosopher, socialist, and naturalist Herbert Spencer (1820-1903). The authors claim that his philosophies, more than those of anyone else, influenced the thinking of the American businessman up to the days of Roosevelt's New Deal.

Management, itself, continues to evolve. Historically, where do we start looking at the process? A sociology timeline suggests that the *industrial revolution* began about 1750. The ideas for democratic management had their birth in the ashes of both the American and the French Revolutions which occurred a few years after the industrial revolution began. The *geography* in which this took place centered in England, Germany, France, and America, nations that have continued to be power players in world affairs up to the present time.

History reveals the role of research in the progress of management. The "Hawthorne Studies," which began in the late 1920s is a prime example. In Chicago, at the Hawthorne plant of AT&T's Western Electric manufacturing facility, studies detailed the psychological impact on workers when variables such as lighting were changed. The bottom line of these experiments was to show evidence that production improves when workers are recognized—in whatever form.

It is more than interesting that the same Hawthorne Works was the place where statistical quality control was first put to practical use with Walter A. Shewhart, W. Edwards Deming, Harold F. Dodge, and Joseph M. Juran all part of the cast of characters who became known as the "fathers of the quality movement."

Today, we read that Deming and Juran are considered two of the most influential persons of the 20th century and that Peter Drucker is listed as one of the past century's most important writers.

We believe it is more than coincidence that Jewish psychologists leaving Nazi Germany, such as Maslow, were the same individuals who gave understanding to the behavioral approach to management, which has been the basis for the emphasis on the *human element* in this field of study.

World War II became a political event that determined which approach to the governing of people would become most dominant in the second half of the 20th century. It had a significant bearing on how management evolved. For example, operations research emerged out of WW II, as did the use of computers. The rebirth of Western Germany and Japan highlighted successful management styles, especially the importance of quality as a competitive advantage—and the need for the total commitment of leadership.

The influence of management was crossing national borders.

YOU ARE MAKING HISTORY

The behavioral scientist is interested in social history as it related to political geography, political science, and economics in the distribution of power and wealth—not to mention the impact on people from a cultural, psychological, and social viewpoint. From studying history as a discipline, we discover what disruptions (i.e. changes) have been brought about by which events and why. Remember, the behavioral scientist is forever the observer, developing theories, and trying to offer scientific explanation.

People engaged in *making history* have moved their agendas, their armies, their might to change events, knowing that their time on earth is limited—that power and influence are fleeting—but caring very little what behavioral scientists might think.

Managers and leaders, who would do well learning the lessons of the behavioral scientists, have an agenda more like people who *make* history. They are busy forging ahead with their agendas, leaving little time for mere observation and theories.

Both the rulers of government and the managers of people are held (sooner or later) accountable. The professors, like our senators in the Congress, spend a great deal of time in debate, and do not hold themselves (nor do others) answerable.

THE FIVE PERSPECTIVES

In an informative book that we highly recommend, *Management—Challenges for the 21st Century*, author Pamela Lewis (and others) present five separate perspectives on management which have evolved over the years:

1. The Classical Perspective
This began in the 1880s and, in some form, continues to this day. It has three sub-fields:

- Scientific management—focusing on the productivity of the individual worker.
- Administrative management—functions such as planning, organizing, leading, coordinating, and controlling.
- Bureaucratic management—dealing with the overall organizational system, based on policies, procedures, and a clear division of labor.

2. The Behavioral Perspective
This started about 1920 and its effects are still felt.

As standards of living began to rise and workers conditions improved, employees began to influence managerial decisions. The powerful labor movements played a huge role in this.

3. The Quantitative Perspective
This viewpoint sprung up in the late 1940s, after WW II.

Borrowing heavily on scientific management approaches, it makes significant use of statistics, mathematics, and other such techniques in (1) decision making, (2) measurable criteria, (3) quantitative models, and (4) computers. As the authors point out, "This has expanded into linear programming, network models, queuing theory, game theory, inventory models, and statistical decision theory."

4. The Systems Perspective

Coming into vogue in the early 1950s, was what is known as "systems analysis." This is where the organization is viewed in relationship to three building blocks:

- Inputs—including materials, workers, capital, land, equipment, customers, and information.
- Outputs—this usually consists of some physical commodity or intangible service or information that is desired by the customers or those who use the system.
- Transformational—the process by which inputs are converted to outputs.

5. The Contingency Perspective

This came along in the 1960s with the theory that there is no best approach to managing an organization. The leadership becomes acquainted with the several perspectives and applies them according to the circumstance or situation.

LESSONS TO LEARN

History provides the story of *power* in the hands of man. It is often a shameful account of the abuse of power, the arrogance of man, and the lack of consideration for both present and future generations. Yet, the manager will find many applicable lessons here.

In summary, we believe the countless stories of power, domination, repression, and general disregard for one's fellowman should alert the modern day manager to the consequence of these actions. Sooner or later, people who are suppressed will find a way to revolt. A workforce with only revenge to past misdeeds is not going to be a high performance work group, so a leader needs cooperation and results.

If it has happened before, we find it may well happen again. This is often referred to as the "Lessons of History."

We say that history repeats itself—in political dogmas, religion, governments, nations, and in organizations of all kinds. We know that, at the same time, evolution is taking place so that things will never quite be the same. But the lessons of the past are vital keys in making decisions for the the future.

Notes for your Playbook

* History is best learned when presented in the form of stories.

- Be careful of those who rewrite history to promote their own bias or agenda.
- Have a working knowledge of social history and how it has evolved.
- Be aware of the various perspectives of management.
- Leaders read of past events and ask, "What can I learn from this?"
- From studying history as a discipline, we discover what changes have been brought about by which events and why.
- The lessons of yesterday are vital in making decisions that affect today and tomorrow.

DISCIPLINE #6

POLITICAL SCIENCE

*Treat 'em like dogs, and you'll have
dogs' work and dogs' actions. Treat 'em like
men, and you'll have men's works.*
– Harriet Beecher Stowe

Power, as applied to Political Science, makes it the most dominant, while at the same time the most elusive of the Ten Disciplines. People with power, similar to those with money feel that if you have it, you don't need to flaunt or talk about it. Power exists in all organizations—whether in the forefront or the background.

It appears in a number of forms, and it can be said that power lives in "two different houses." Most commonly, it is thought to reside with the "mansions on the hillside," where it indeed does. But it also has its home down in the level of the city, where the air is not as fresh and the dwellings are not as large.

In organizations, since there are constant shifts going on, power is a ceaseless moving of the sands. We are continually examining and questioning, "Who is 'in control' of 'whose' destiny?"

Because authoritarianism is the most prevalent leadership style, it is easy to see why managers don't want to let go of their turf and empower others. This affects their ability to delegate.

Power may be positive, negative, or neutral, yet it is constantly present, and its skills must be in a manager's toolbox.

According to John Kotter, former professor of organizational behavior at Harvard Business School: "Managers who have little skill at or inclination toward power-oriented behavior sometimes remain in low-level managerial jobs throughout their careers, with few subordinates and few coordination responsibilities." And he adds, "Most workers fail to realize that management can't reach its goals without the cooperation of the entire workforce. An appreciation for the impact of authority is key to understanding how the managerial process works."

To understand how power interacts with the leadership system, when managers attempt to change an organization and those in control of the resources are determined to retain the status quo, the battle lines are drawn. It is a classic confrontation between the retention of power and the exercise of leadership. Stories of such conflicts appear continually in business publications.

Political science investigates the nature, source, organization, and administration of power and control in human society. In this very definition we find two key management words: *power* and *control*. They form the core foundation of any system of government, as well as the keystones to a manager's philosophy toward his duties. Both are very significant to the manager's behavior, style, and relationship with associates.

LESSONS FROM A PRESIDENT

There are many excellent role models for American Leadership, but we believe it is personified in the life of Abraham Lincoln perhaps better than any other individual we could name.

Lincoln certainly demonstrated leadership qualities throughout his life, but it is in his presidency, with the future of our nation at stake, that we come to grips with the depth of his ability to cope and to use wisdom in his judgments and decisions.

First, it is important to note that in the events surrounding the Civil War, Lincoln had absolutely no personal or potential gain at stake. He was solely interested in finding a way to preserve the union—survival.

More recent history focusing on the war as a struggle to abolish slavery is placing the emphasis on a secondary issue which is very significant, but at the time of Lincoln's presidency it was not the major focal point.

Second, his success or failure as a leader would determine the survival of the United States. In an earlier struggle, George Washington was one of many patriots whose commitment and skills birthed this nation in the first place. For Washington, failure would have been seen as treason and perhaps resulted in the loss of his life.

Many of Lincoln's decisions had to be all or nothing; he could not straddle the fence or be indecisive. Everything he did had multiple issues attached. In some ways he was fighting the politics of the north as much as the army and culture of the south—there were many enemies on all sides. He had very few, other than his family, rooting for his personal success, but that is not the goal he was seeking.

Lincoln was a family man. And since many of the battles took place close to home, he could remain a father to his children, and to his countrymen. These all brought many problems to his doorstep.

President Lincoln did not hide in the solace of his office or behind his cabinet. He went out into the battlefield to talk to the generals and to the troops, and could see the light from their campfires at night from his Washington base. He was neither popular nor understood. In many ways it was only his faith, humor, and perspective that carried him through. While Lincoln exhibited values and integrity, he was not truly appreciated for these attributes.

There were many who wanted to seize his power, but no one had an adequate awareness of the weight of his burden. He, who believed so much in the democratic principles on which this nation was founded, had to make potentially unlawful autocratic decisions to save the union. It required strong action, and he was up to the task—knowing both when and how to do this.

Lincoln lacked the comfort of a supportive team, but through his inner strength and strong convictions made many of these difficult decisions in virtual isolation. One of the few places in which he could get away was across the street at the telegraph office which received a constant stream of messages from the field. Each day, it became the media event for him.

Despite these heavy burdens, he retained his light-hearted disposition, continued to be a people person and never considered "growing an ego" to fit his large physical frame.

He was insightful—which is discernable from the words of his immortal Gettysburg Address. In addition, Lincoln was his "own person." His faithful wife, Mary, influenced his life but she did not make decisions for him. Despite extreme political pressure, he was able to sort out the facts from rumor and stick to the truth.

The end came just five days after General Robert E. Lee, commander of the Confederate Army of Northern Virginia, surrendered to Lieutenant General Ulysses S. Grant of the Union Army. On April 14, 1865, at Ford's Theatre in Washington, D. C, where Lincoln, his wife, and friends were seated in the Presidential Box watching the stage play, *Our American Cousin*, the unthinkable happened. Well-known actor, John Wilkes Booth, a Confederate sympathizer, entered the box and, at close range, shot the President. Lincoln gave the supreme sacrifice.

SHORT TERM VS. LONG TERM POWER

In this book, we have made several references to the wide use of a dictatorial leadership style (which is quite the opposite of Lincoln's). While it gives short-term power to a

CEO, executive, or manager, they will certainly pay for it in the long run with decreased morale, higher turnover, and slowing productivity. Never doubt the fact that employees also hold power, and can exert it by withholding their best efforts or deciding to "just get by."

Is this the atmosphere in which a leader wants to work?

Since there can be "perceived inequities" by employees in any organization, how do we address them?

In today's "entitlement culture," the fine line you have to walk is to make sure there is accountability for all and that you fully communicate the company's vision, values, norms, beliefs, and expected behaviors. Unfortunately (or perhaps fortunately) you may have to weed out those with "victim" thinking—which can spring up in employees entering the workforce from a wide variety of cultural or educational backgrounds.

AVOIDING CHAOS

One of the questions we are frequently asked is, "How can management avoid employee chaos—or even workplace anarchy?"

Here is one of the major keys. If you are in a position of authority and witness something out of place—and those performing the act see that you noticed—immediately acknowledge this. If you fail to do so (each and every time), you will not be perceived as a leader and additional turmoil may follow. When a named leader or manager becomes an "avoider," no one is actually in control.

One of the points we drive home in our seminars is that if you are the owner, CEO, or president of a firm, everything you say is significant.

There will be times when a "trust issue" needs to be resolved. Again, this cannot be postponed.

- If it is a personal issue, deal with it one-on-one.
- If it is a group concern, address it with the entire group.
- If one or two on the management team cannot be trusted, you will have to replace them to gain the confidence and respect of the others.

You must process the issue—not ignore it.

SPOTTING A POWERFUL PERSON

Robert L. Dilenschneider, founder and chairman of a global public relations and communications firm, wrote the bestseller, *Power and Influence*. He asks, "What criteria set the powerful apart from all the others? Besides their competence, it is their ability to generate ideas, their sense of mission, their self-confidence, and their need for achievement, that is, getting something done. How can you spot a powerful person? Look at his or her results. Are these people directly or indirectly responsible for getting a lot of things done? And especially, are they somehow responsible for getting a lot done through others?"

Then he adds, "What is it that these powerful people are

trying to get done? It's nearly axiomatic that powerful individuals seek to exert influence outside themselves. But, this is also true for organizations. Power for the individual in an organization is the ability to influence the direction of an organization that has a real impact."

A major goal should be to end the isolation that so often exists between employees and management.

Sure, there are standards, procedures, and boundaries that must be insisted upon, you need to develop a system and make sure employees are comfortable within its limits.

One of the great dangers faced by corporate boards is to choose a company leader based on their outward confidence and "power" without knowing what's "under the hood."

We encourage you to find a copy of *The Prince*, written in the 16th century by Niccolo Machiavelli, an Italian politician and writer. Today, the term "Machiavellianism" is used to describe a person's tendency to be unemotional, selfish, and manipulative. You probably can think of at least one narcissistic boss you've had somewhere down the road who falls into this category.

PROMOTIONS AND REWARDS

One of the most discussed topics in enterprises of all sizes involves the politics of promotions and rewards. Let's face it, a real bugaboo for labor and management alike has been the dreaded annual review.

More and more companies are getting rid of this review and turning to other procedures. One popular alternative is called "Catalytic Coaching." This is where you say to an employee face to face what you would normally comment upon behind their back. It's a series of meetings, where the worker shares with the boss their present situation and where they want to be. Then for the next meeting, the manager prepares feedback, discussing strength, areas for improvement, and recommendations for development. Then comes an exchange where the employee presents what he or she is going to be doing over the next several months.

Gary Markle, a human resources consultant to many Fortune 500 companies, developed the concept and describes it as "an integrated system of performance and management designed to facilitate a constructive partnership between a manager and employee. It is built around frank, open, and constructive feedback and a shared desire for each individual to achieve his ultimate potential."

Since advancement or other rewards could come at any time, for many companies and individuals it has led to much smoother progress.

DISCOVERING POWER BASES

Many CEO's have been brought into organizations by corporate boards, and the new leader has no earthly idea what the lay of the land looks like. Suddenly, they are treading lightly through a minefield that is littered with "power" factions and hidden agendas.

The only way to survive in such an arena is to have a friendly series of one-on-ones with each member of your management, hopefully to determine who is with you and who is not. You must also realize there is probably a "sub-culture" which has its own management team that mimics the *actual* management team. You need to deal with them —individually and in group meetings. It's absolutely essential that you find out who holds the real power in these groups and work with those men and women to reach a state of *shared fate*. Unfortunately, anyone not truly on the team must go.

There are occasions (and we have experienced them personally) where an acquisition takes place and you "inherit" a leadership and management team that knows nothing about how you have operated successfully for years. They believe they hold all the answers going forward. Both teams need to take a deep breath and be flexible, adaptable, and willing to listen.

If someone tells you, "We're about to merge with (so and so) company), don't believe them. In reality, there are no mergers, only acquisitions. It is well known that when culture meets change, culture generally wins—or should we say *always* wins.

In most scenarios, the only elements that save the day are the clarity of the company's values and mission statement.

THE LOYALTY FACTOR

If you talk to leaders at length about what they look for in building their management team, one phrase will likely crop up again and again: "I want people who are loyal."

That sounds good, and when you are building an enterprise it is absolutely essential, but there comes a time when you must either expand or perish. If you only have "loyal" employees to choose from for new positions, you may discover they don't have the business acumen, skill sets, or knowledge base to fit the new job descriptions and the complexities that are required for growth.

What to do? You always find a place for loyal workers, but you select future managers based on what they can bring to the table. Hopefully, they will turn out to be loyal, too.

GOVERNMENT VS. CORPORATE

In studying the discipline of political science as it relates to leadership, it is worth comparing how power struggles in government correspond to those in the private sector.

In the corporate world, if leaders don't perform they are usually removed (however, there are times when ownership and performance get mixed up in this equation).

In government, as many have observed (and there are plenty of examples), responsible statesmen (and stateswomen) are not always appreciated; in fact, they are often ignored. But as long as those in authority have favorable press, lying is acceptable, even winked at. As a result, deceit becomes the norm—and we are dealing with power vs. power, as if that's all that truly matters.

INTERSECTING INFLUENCES

The noted German-American, Leo Strauss, who spent most of his career as a political science professor at the University of Chicago, points out in his monumental work, *History of Political Philosophy*, that two major influences have guided the direction of thought down through the years:

1. How much of our beliefs are determined by the gods or those forces which are greater than mortal man.
2. How much of our philosophical thought changed as we discovered more of the natural laws and sciences that were able to prove such things as the world is round, not flat.

Again, we see how studies in areas such as geography and philosophy intersect with other disciplines.

In terms of political science, the form of government that is at the top of the pyramid exerts an absolute influence on the work of the manager. If leaders think they can do their job in China, Russia, Iran, or Cuba today exactly as it is performed in the United States, they are delusional. Of course, we would like to believe that leaders in all countries have the right to guide their companies in a democratic way, but far too often politics trumps management.

It must also be noted that in America there is a cry that grows louder and louder each year regarding the over-legislative and burdensome laws that are becoming a rope around the neck of business.

Power has been called, "the worst of all addictions." But used wisely, when needed, and accompanied by caring, encouragement, and love, it can elevate a leader—and an organization—to new heights.

Notes for you Playbook

- There are always power factors at work in leadership and management.
- Political science investigates the nature, source, and administration of power and control in society.
- Abraham Lincoln was successful because he was mission driven rather than having a personality-based agenda.
- Heavy-handed, authoritative, politically-based leaders may have short term gains, but long term failures.
- Avoid chaos by quickly acknowledging and addressing workplace issues.
- Regarding promotion and rewards, be aware of alternatives to the dreaded employee annual review.
- Look for loyalty, but appoint managers for their skill and expertise.

DISCIPLINE #7

ECONOMICS

*I learned more about economics from one South
Dakota dust storm than I did in all my years in college.*
— Hubert Humphrey

As a young plant manager in Rosemount, Minnesota (Jacobs), I found grievance meetings with the union representative to be extremely frustrating. It took some time, but finally I discovered my answer. Since the union was the grieving party, they made the presentation. The nature of the proposition was always the same—a specific clause in the contract was cited as having been violated. There was no discussion on the subject, just a finger pointing to the wording.

The specifics often changed, but the issue was always the same—money. Someone didn't get what they thought they deserved and felt slighted. It was interesting that as each of these complaints moved up the procedure chain, they all seemed to disappear. It became clear that these issues were being kept in the bag for negotiating purposes.

This is a prime example of a "single tool" approach to

management. In this case, everything centered around finances.

Let me give you another example.

As a young industrial engineer, my department head would use the expense account as his single tool. In no other manner did he show his authority. But in this one area, he would discuss what you had for dinner, question buying a bottle of wine for the table, debate mileage between points, and where you might have chosen to stay. In the end, the dollars stayed pretty much the same, but the arrangement of the expenses had gone from actual to preferred—so as to "look right."

In one particular case, I had worked in Washington, Pennsylvania, for three weeks and had not submitted a bill for motel expenses. However, I did turn in daily mileage of 60 miles, but only a small amount a day for meals. In short, the expense account did not "look right." I was engaged at the time, staying at the home of my fiancé, where I had breakfast and dinner, but did have a 60 mile round trip each day. My lunch was very inexpensive because the company had a semi-cafeteria that had a low daily charge. Together, we sat down and "built" a more appropriate looking expense account that actually cost the company more money, not less.

EGGS FROM THE GOLDEN GOOSE

My first assignments with Brockway Glass, both as a summer laborer and later as a graduate engineer involved

102

long hours, physical toil, tough working conditions, and low pay. However, for the most part, we all seemed pretty happy.

Standards and expectations were difficult and high; morale was good. *We* were building something—a company —together.

As the industry matured and the opening of plants changed to an industry with excess capacity, our corporation started to copy the practices of others: incentive opportunity for managers, stock options, nearly no weekend work, higher pay, newer company cars, and so on. But over time, both morale and productivity went down, not up. Why? Because the focus became one of who would get more than someone else.

In due time, the eggs from the Golden Goose no longer satisfied; only by killing the goose [selling the company] and having the stock price escalate from $39/share to a sale price of $60/share was the appetite for greed satisfied for a short while.

WHAT TOOLS ARE NEEDED?

A specific style of leadership was made popular in the last century by Harold Geneen when he was CEO at ITT Corporation. Monthly, his division heads would travel to headquarters with their "bluebooks" and defend their monthly results. That too was basically a single tool meeting.

If your operating income [Year-To-Date] was on or better than budget, you were out of the barrel for the time being.

If not, you were in hot water. When interest rates hit 20% in 1980, a second tool was added—the amount of working capital on the balance sheet.

Companies that measure "cost centers" on the basis of cost and budget without regard for revenue or activity are further examples of this one-tool approach.

In many surveys when employees are asked to respond to the questions: *What is our purpose? What is our objective?* they give a single answer: "To make a profit."

Since the management axiom of "what gets rewarded gets done" is true, this is the single area that is targeted. Other areas often come up short.

A single focus on current profit will actually work—for a while. The expectations of all the stakeholders of an organization [for profit] are in the form of money in the short term. Pay checks, dividends, taxes, supplier payments, low prices to customers, and the paying of interest are all examples of needs satisfied by the generating of immediate profits.

However, since most companies want to be around forever, long term expectations become more diverse and complicated. Now we are facing issues such as stock appreciation for shareholders, job security and promotions for employees, new products and services for customers, permanent partnerships with suppliers and customers, good neighbor policies, job growth for the community and for the government's interests, and so it goes.

Single tool management is not adequate to deliver all of these expectations. Additional tools may help, but still leave us without the right answers. It is here we must turn to relationship management by negotiation and collaboration with our stakeholders hammering out goals to meet all of the expectations, then setting up priorities to determine which wheel gets greased when we come up short, or who gets the extra hay when we have a surplus.

We also must develop a set of values that keep us on track. Profit without virtue may be very short lived. But profit with values will provide the foundation for a long term successful stay in the communities of our choice.

UNION ISSUES

Without question, the success of a company must be the vision of both labor and management. Unfortunately, there have been far too many "breakdowns" between these two factions over the years.

For example, in the early 1980s, the Caterpillar corporation was losing $1 million a day due to a sharp downturn in demand and increased competition with its Japanese rival, Komatsu. The layoffs led to major strikes by the United Auto Workers that lasted several years—until union workers agreed to come back even without a contract. During the time, Caterpillar embarked on what is called the "Southern Strategy"—building plants in "right to work" states.

There are two sides to every story. For example, in 2012, when one of Caterpillar's local northern unions went on strike, it resulted in a future six-year wage freeze. The striking workers, however, were angry that because of record profits the year before, the CEO of the corporation received a 60 percent salary increase.

One of the major economic stories of the past century has been the fact that labor union membership in the United States stood at 21 million in 1979, and had fallen to 14.5 million by 2013.

MASTERING ECONOMIC THEORY

An important asset in building relationship skills is to start to master the message of the Ten Disciplines. The collaboration of money capital, human capital, natural resources, and technology, in a positive growth atmosphere, can far outdistance a company using only a single yardstick of profit for success. If you do all the other things right, the profits will come. There's a biblical passage that conveys the same meaning: the farmer who sowed his seed "on good soil...it came up and yielded a crop, a hundred times more than was sown" (Luke 8).

Basically, economics is the discipline that deals with the creation, production, and consumption of wealth, and the means of supplying material resources.

Every leader needs to master economic theory and fiscal accountability. They should know:

• How to read, interpret, and act on the information from the income statement and the balance sheet.

- How to understand the impact of cash management, working capital, inventory, and debt.
- How to develop a working model of their particular business and develop a system of predicting future results (6 months, 12 months, etc.).

Those in leadership should spend time getting up to speed on how economics has shaped our nation, our enterprises, and why its principles are worth applying today.

Here is a brief overview, which we hope will spark your curiosity enough to begin reading some of the economic texts referenced at the end of this book.

- During the millennia from the 5th to the 15th centuries, the world experienced the medieval economy that was basically an agricultural society. Problems were solved according to custom and tradition.
- In medieval times, the church was the basic social institution and the deliberate accumulation of wealth was considered sinful. But, because of social stratification, some were allowed to enjoy luxuries, including, kings, princes, nobles, and church dignitaries.
- Martin Luther's Protestant Reformation began in 1517 when he posted the "95 Theses" on the Castle Church door in Wittenburg, Germany. There were many repercussions, one being that wealth-building was no longer seen as a sin.

- In the mid-1600s, Jean-Baptiste Colbert, the French finance minister, pioneered state control of the economy. It was Colbert who said, "The art of taxation consists in so plucking the goose as to obtain the largest amount of feathers with the smallest amount of hissing."
- In 1665, William Petty, an English economist, was the first to measure gross domestic product (GDP).
- The same year that the Declaration of Independence was signed, 1776, economics became a scholarly discipline in the new nation when Adam Smith published *The Wealth of Nations.*
- "The Economist," a London-based magazine devoted to free trade, was first published in 1843.
- In 1867, Karl Marx tried to proclaim that capitalism was doomed. In his book, *Capital: Critique of Political Economy,* Marx predicted a future of government-run socialism. Fast-forward one century and one-third of the world lived in nations where the Marxian doctrine was the law of the land.
- Two years later, thousands of businesses were ruined when financiers Jay Gould and James Fisk tried to capture the gold market.
- In 1883, the world's first credit union was formed by German economist Franz Herman Shulze-Delizsch.
- When the Great Depression hit the United States in the late 1920s, some thought Marx was right. Thirty billion in paper value was wiped out in one day.

- In 1933, the U.S. went off the gold standard.
- Beginning in the 1930s, British economist John Maynard Keynes became a high-profile proponent of government intervention in economic matters.
- In the 1970s, Milton Friedman argued that changes in the money supply precede changes in overall economic conditions.
- During 2008-2009, because of low introductory rates, many homeowners were unable to pay their mortgages, causing the "housing bubble" to burst. It prompted a recession in the United States, with repercussions worldwide.

TAKING THE LONG VIEW

Today, the distribution of wealth remains an economic, political, philosophical, sociological, psychological, and mathematical puzzle. It is the underlying common denominator of political systems.

All systems of wealth distribution have their pros and cons. It is safe to say that until the "private man" was able to keep some of his own *harvest* or *production*, there was little incentive—other than avoiding the threat of death for him to labor or toil for the wealth of others.

Countries (cultures) may look at short term and long term results differently. In recent years the impact of Wall Street, the leveraged buyouts and other factors, have driven the United States to an emphasis on short term results [i.e. instant gratification]. Other strong economic countries such as Germany and Japan are taking the long view far more than we are.

Our country was built on looking toward the future, but many feel this current trend will be disastrous in the longer term. This is why managers and leaders need to have a handle on applied economics.

"HURRY UP! HURRY UP!"

The question is often asked, "What is productivity?"

To many in positions of authority, it appears that they have been led to believe that if you frown or stare at people *hard* and *long* enough, it will magically increase productivity. To intensify this effort, sometimes "work study" people are sent to observe, analyze, and write down every movement of individual employees, with the intention of finding ways for the person to do the job in less time. This has been going on since the beginning of the 20th century, when Frederick Winslow Taylor, a mechanical engineer, introduced the method of breaking a job into components that could each be measured. We have experienced first hand what it means to be brought into a plant as "Efficiency Experts."

In the play and movie, *Pajama Game*, the song "Hurry Up Hurry Up" is written about such an expert and his need to constantly "save time." He tells the women at the pajama factory, "Seconds are ticking...Can't waste time."

It's no wonder that even today, workers in plants and

offices soon learn to hate and mistrust these types of managers. As a leader, you need to be aware of what works, and what doesn't. Make sure you are acquainted with the motivation and economic theories developed by Douglas McGregor in the 1960s while he taught at the MIT's Sloan School of Management. His Theory X and Theory Y are still being discussed.

- **Theory X**—This assumes the manager believes employees are inherently lazy, dislike work, and will avoid it if they can. This leads to restrictive supervision and an atmosphere that is punitive in nature.
- **Theory Y**—This assumes the manager believes employees are ambitious, exercise self-control and are self-motivated. Given the right environment, workers will engage in creative problem-solving and will move the organization forward.

It's been proven again and again that productivity is the highest when the people doing the job are trained, skilled, and motivated without constantly having individuals checking, bothering, and worrying them. This is why a skilled work force on the night shift can often run rings around the productivity from the dayshift.

When is output the lowest? It can be in the same "off shift" when no one is around to oversee the work or efforts of the employees. However, in this case the people doing the work may be unskilled, untrained, and certainly unmotivated —doing little if anything unless there is direct supervision to watch over them every moment.

The number one factor in these comparisons is whether or not workers have the necessary training to succeed. But we cannot ignore the predisposition of managers toward the work force.

Games Employees Play

At some point, most tasks become repetitive, which for normally intelligent people means they become bored on the job. A manager or leader who leans on employees to do more of the same ol' same ol' leaves the worker with one motive—to get even.

If there is no one around to observe, employees can even the score by various means of sabotage, which really isn't much fun. The process can become an active game of us (worker) vs. them (manager). The game starts out by those in authority feeling they have the necessary leverage to push the productivity accelerator to the floor and watch the results. But, in fact, the real leverage is with the people doing the job(s) who, by non-verbal means, just their body language, put into process an entire new set of problems that they have created for just such purposes. They suddenly produce an aura of considerable concern, which for some reason results in most of the productive work being halted until they are able to share the problem with one of the "authority types" who will be called over to help, assist, and make a decision about what to do about the issue.

In far too many cases the authority person does not have a clue, so eventually, by clever manipulation on the part of the "worker," the supervisor, manager, or department head will ask: "What do you think?"

GOTCHA! The score at that point is 1-0 in favor of the employee, and the game resumes.

At this juncture, a committee is often formed and a meeting is arranged to study these mysterious events. The score is now 2-0, and the rout is on.

The Japanese apparently overcame this dilemma by the creation of something called "quality circles" in which the input from all impacted parties was used for decision making. But when incorporating it into our plants and offices, we often forgot to involve our top managers, who were too busy for such things.

We laugh at Dilbert cartoons, the satirical humor about a white-collar micromanaged office, but there is no rational reason for the management function to become the source of such ridicule. Regardless, many of Dilbert's punch-lines ring true.

THE KEYS TO PRODUCTIVITY

So how do we *get* productivity?

• Provide the resources and up-to-date equipment.

- Provide the environment: good working conditions where trust and positive recognition are prevalent.
- Provide the training: people must have skills.

But what about the workers who refuse to take advantage of a good situation and insist on "screwing up"—no matter what. Unfortunately, these are the *irregulars* who need to be culled from the workforce. However, before you rush to get rid of anyone, make sure they truly are the problem and they have no intention of letting you help fix their shortcomings.

In balancing the budget, one of the biggest mistakes a leader can make is to start cutting costs without worker input. Instead, call the workforce together and show them what competitors can do in terms of price, quality, and delivery. Then ask, "Can we find a way to match and then beat them? If not, what is our next move?"

You may be surprised when the people doing the job suggest a change in their pay, hours, methods, etc. They are just as concerned about survival (their own) as is the management.

Secondly, share results and measurements. Change the game to one of mutual cooperation. But remember to discuss the results—good or bad—in a timely manner.

PUTTING THE PIECES TOGETHER

A leader is required to make hundreds, even thousands of decisions annually. Whether the issue deals with relationships, attitudes, health benefits, productivity, or a dozen other factors, there is always an underlying economic impact involved.

In the words of the noted Paul Saumelson, the first American to win the Nobel Prize in Economic Sciences, "Economics covers all kinds of topics. But at the core it is devoted to understanding the way businesses, households, and governments behave; it attempts to figure out the 1001 puzzles of everyday life."

When you master this discipline, you'll be able to put the pieces together.

Notes for your Playbook

- A "single tool" leadership approach seldom works.
- Profit with values provides the foundation for long term success.
- In dealings between labor and management, economic survival requires relational skills.
- Today's leaders need to know how economics has shaped our nation and its enterprises.
- Productivity is best when leaders have faith in the abilities and creativity of its workers.
- Leadership should provide the right resources, the right environment, and the right training.
- Always involve employees in the process of balancing the company budget.

DISCIPLINE #8

ANTHROPOLOGY

Always remember that you are
absolutely unique. Just like everyone else.
– Margaret Mead

In consulting with the CEO of a rather large corporation in the Midwest, the confused executive asked, "What happens that kills the spirit of the people we hire? We have the ability and resources to bring in and promote the best talent in the industry. We pay well, offer a complete package of benefits, provide training opportunities, and have a pleasant working environment. What else could they want? Why don't they continue to grow? What turns them off?"

Here's what often takes place. The culture, which continues to be "keep the boss happy," has far too many in the management ranks concentrating on pointing out employees who are doing something wrong. Audits and reviews by human resources should be viewed as partners in "getting things right"—but they aren't. Instead they are seen as a sort of Gestapo. Their findings, with or without foundation, become a law unto themselves. Pardon our expression, but the system stinks!

You can try to change the organizational chart, decentralize, analyze, and empower, but until the culture changes, you're just spinning your wheels.

It's a shame when encounters with management are remembered by employees by their negative content far more than the "once in awhile" positive recognition. What is the result? People become resentful and lose what trust they might have had. They also grow defensive, so much so that CYA becomes the system of each worker.

Often, this style of management is coupled with imposing numbers which may or may not be relevant. Cooperation is scarce; competition reigns. Workers are continually wondering, "Who are the spies?"

In this atmosphere, where everyone (except the person responsible) is questioned, resentment is born.

In a labor market filled with those from companies who have downsized and who have learned to keep their mouths shut, it is easy to find chameleons to fill your management ranks.

SPECIAL AGENTS

Other signs that a workforce is falling apart is when those who are faithfully doing their jobs are not asked for their participation or their opinions. It's as if a "secret mission" is underway and the study teams are filled with special agents.

The team looking at the situation may say they only want

to reflect the company's best interests, when in fact their loyalty is only to themselves. But this clueless group resorts to the one thing they think they understand: costs. How can we do it for less?"

Who usually loses in this process? Those doing the tasks. And who generally wind up getting a raise for their recommendations? Those who imposed the cost cuts.

There's a place for reducing expenses, but only when done in a manner that will truly bring improvement—such as changing the system, revising the methods, or obtaining new resources. But just reducing headcounts or wages without having adequate knowledge of the process will guarantee failure, not success.

Perhaps it's time to ask: *Are there as many people analyzing the numbers as there are generating them?*

Other components come into play, including the working environment and "the way we do things around here." The culture is dominated, not just by the formal organization, but more by the informal organization.

It is the anthropology of the enterprise that helps shape the person in charge. If the new leader chooses to reject the past then he/she is setting up the battle between change and culture—and again, culture normally wins.

WHO IS WATCHING?

At its nucleus, anthropology is primarily concerned with

observation. As Yoga Berra once said, "You can observe a lot by just watching."

Today, companies are hiring people whose sole purpose is to improve a product or service by closely monitoring employees on the job—how they interact with technology, equipment, and each other.

While anthropology is defined as the scientific study of human beings, it involves several distinct, yet interconnected, scientific fields including:

- Human evolution—studying fossils of man.
- Physical anthropology—classifying geographical populations and their changes over time.
- Archeology—prehistory.
- Cultural anthropology—a society's social groups, beliefs, arts, symbols, customs, values, institutions, languages, inventions, even their technology.

The study of the religious side of man is both a part of anthropology and philosophy.

CULTURE SHOCK!

It's interesting that we are born as a "blank slate," without any knowledge of a particular culture. We learn this by listening, observing, and interacting with those around us. Soon, we start imitating the behaviors we see. Academics call this "enculturation"—and these values and habits are passed on through the generations.

Societies are held together because of what the members have in common. This is reflected in such things as their religious practices, the foods they eat, their relationships, the arts they embrace, and the way they conduct business.

At the other end of the pendulum from enculturation is "assimilation"—which is supposed to take place when people from different backgrounds move to locations separate from their own.

However, reality sets in when you talk to officials of our major cities and they show you a map and point to various areas: "Here's where the Asians live. Over here it's predominantly Hispanic. This is an African-American enclave. And that side of town is primarily middle-class white."

On the job, however, it can be an entirely different story. The term "culture shock" can certainly apply to what many leaders have faced with a multi-cultural workforce. This is why it is absolutely essential to have a handle on diversity.

NEW TERRITORY

A corporate leader in today's global market may be reassigned, with very little notice, to any spot on the globe. For those of us who have moved a number of times within the United States, we can only imagine the cultural contrast in landing in some far distant city—surrounded by a new language and strange customs.

One of the quickest and surest ways for a new manager to

gain social acceptance in a foreign environment is to show both an interest and appreciation in his/her new cultural setting. This will involve embracing local sports, leisure activities, shopping, food, and many other areas.

Since you are in "their" territory, don't make the mistake of degrading their lifestyle in any way.

THE DIVERSITY FACTOR

The reason we need to learn as much as possible about the culture is to be able to unite the separate threads of society and backgrounds into a strong cord. From a leader's point of view we might give this a fancy name such as "Optimizing of differences for maximum effectiveness." Or perhaps, "The Win-Win of Diversity." This burning social and political reality of pluralism is both an issue in anthropology and sociology.

The problem for the manager is that each and every group (i.e. race, nationality, religion, sexual preference, political party, etc.) has its own agenda. While the manager must give a certain amount of respect to what may be the driving force of a particular individual, the real task is to direct the diverse groups to the mission of the organization during the hours they spend in its employment.

WORK FLOW

Have you ever watched a flowing brook? When the water

drifts into a rock, it causes a ripple—and the water must change its course.

People in managerial positions often become impediments to the work flow. They do this by looking to find something wrong, interrupting the work by asking unrelated questions to remind people of their authority, or finding some other method to be a hindrance.

In an organization, if it happens to be the busy season, there is a generous amount of meaningful work for everyone to do—every day. This eliminates the tendency for "pretend" or "make work." It also takes away the need to stretch projects so they take longer to complete. The flip side of managing during boom times is not to exert too much pressure or to incur excessive overtime costs. Delivery dates must be realistic and must be kept. It is a chance to focus almost singularly on outstanding customer service.

We have seen times when managers were so busy that lower level "crew leaders" (hourly workers) were running the day to day activities of the workforce. The flow was as smooth as an orchestra playing in perfect harmony. Why was this possible? Because the crew leaders knew exactly what they were doing, what they wanted to accomplish, how much time they had to finish the assignment, and the individual skills of each of their co-workers.

They realized the importance of being fair and could concentrate totally on the mission at hand without any fear of a managerial person [above them] coming along and causing an impediment. They could also count on a complete backing of their actions. Therefore, their authority, as delicate as it might be, was not being questioned either by those above them or those reporting to them.

The chemistry is provided because the people not only like their tasks, but enjoy working together. This being the case, the hours fly by and employees are able to maintain a high energy level, in spite of long working hours.

THE OBJECTIVE

It is not the work that generally tires people out, it is the frustration—which can be caused by the boss, the system, the policies, or the work environment. The key to eliminating these annoyances is to focus the work group toward one agenda.

- First: Each individual has to be willing to check his/her personal agenda at the door every day.
- Second: It is important that each person knows exactly what the daily objective is.
- Third, it works best if each person is encouraged to participate in how the task will be divided and accomplished.
- Fourth, a few complimentary words throughout the day help immensely.

There have been dozens of books written on the theme of driving fear out of the workplace. It's a serious topic because the "motivation by fear" technique is extremely energy intensive in terms of wearing people out.

On the other hand, a positive chemistry—a camaraderie —develops as the people begin to enjoy working together and accomplishing things in teams or groups. This may include or exclude those in a supervisory position.

It is also worth noting how there are cultural subsets within the same company. One group may focus on pleasing the customers, another on pleasing the boss. Then you find some corporate types focused almost entirely on cost vs. budget, compliance, policy, and procedures.

TRADITIONS! TRADITIONS!

Every organization needs its own traditions and culture. It unites employees and gives them a shared identity and a sense of togetherness.

If some date is unique to your company, create an annual event around it. But there are dozens of ways you can achieve the same positive results. Here are a few examples:

- At a company in New Jersey, every time a team reaches one of their goals, they get to hit a large, loud gong in the office.
- A sales organization in Dallas has an annual pumpkin-carving contest for its employees.
- A Wall Street brokerage firm has "Tacky Tie Tuesday" to see who can wear the most outlandish tie.

- Many businesses hold an annual Christmas party for the children of the employees—with Santa as the special guest.

Never think that celebrating in some unusual manner is a waste of time. Just the opposite; it bonds workers and management together in very special ways.

MEETINGS, DECISIONS, AND YOU

The American manager spends far too much of his/her time in meetings. These sessions come in all sizes and shapes and the meeting of minds around a table at business, school, church, and civic organizations must be considered a part of our culture.

Information is exchanged: sometimes free-wheeling and candid; sometimes very carefully and guarded. At some sessions food is served, but other meetings can be rather spartan. You know the agenda will be short if you are asked to stand.

At work, there are staff meetings, sales meetings, monthly meetings, etc., all for the sake of hoping to improve our performance.

We have to ask: *How many times are real decisions made during these sessions?* Almost never. The reason being that to play out an important decision requires a great deal of behind-the-scenes discussion, the use of influence, the exertion of power, and the negotiation of trade-offs.

Formal labor negotiations are a good example. No important decisions are made at the table. They are only *brought to the table* later.

So why have meetings at all? Communication, collaboration, inclusiveness, tradition.

The chief complaint of many managers is their feeling of "time compression." In today's world, meetings, email, voice mail, and phone calls take up a great deal of the working day. This means the real work must be done at night, or early in the morning.

To be worthwhile, meetings must have an agenda, time limits, a facilitator, and a purpose. That last element is often lacking. The purpose would seem to be to make a decision—something we carefully avoid.

Are there any worthwhile meetings? Yes, if you have a good manager! But in the vast majority of cases, the only real decision that is made is setting the date and time for the next meeting!

FIRST BORNS

There are some who believe that the root causes of many organizational problems are the personality traits that reside in many of our leaders.

If you want some food for thought on this topic, find a copy of Kevin Lehman's, *The Birth Order Book.* There's an intriguing chapter titled, "First Born, First Come, First Served."

He states that the typical characteristics of first born people include "perfectionistic, reliable, conscientious, list makers, well organized, critical, serious, scholarly. And to that list you could add: goal oriented, achiever, well-sacrificing, people pleaser, conservative, supporter of law and order, believer in authority and ritual, legalistic, loyal, self-reliant."

The point Lehman makes is that if you aren't a first-born yourself, you will likely have to deal with one at some point along the line.

THE DIGITAL DIVIDE

If one's personal values conflict with those of the company, trouble is on the horizon. Or, if the culture of the enterprise changes and it doesn't fit the values of the employee, he/she will not be able continue at the same level of effectiveness. There will be too many disconnects.

Strange as it may seem, there are individuals entering the work force who have a dread of technology. They either have not learned a computer or digital skill or feel their personality will somehow get them through. But those days are over.

Since technology is here to stay (and changing by the month), it's up to leadership to make continual high-tech training available to everyone. If there are those still in the workforce who cannot learn these skills, they will either have to be assigned to a job not requiring them or be asked to leave.

ON THE MOUNTAINTOP

Before leaving this discipline, we want to share this analogy.

In ancient times the chosen people of Israel were restless. They were straying from their basic principles and other gods were being worshiped. Their manager was at his wits end. Then God called Moses to come to the mountaintop.

Together they set out to map the current process and study why it was failing. When they were finished, they were so sure of the solution, they set it in stone. As the final words were processed, Moses prepared for the journey down the mountain—lugging his re-engineering report for the people.

When he rounded the final bend of the mountain, he caught a glimpse of the masses with a large golden image that had been shaped by fire. Moses became enraged at their idolatry and threw down the Ten Commandments—which broke into many pieces.

Then he heard a voice: "Mo! It's God. I don't think you approached the situation just right. Come back up the mountain, let's try again."

So together they reviewed the values, applied the lessons, and reduced them to the basics. A little later Moses headed back down the mountain with two new stone scrolls in hand.

This account has been recorded in the book known to many of us as the Bible—a report we have been studying for over 2000 years. The contents may be difficult to master, but it is still very relevant—even for leaders.

Notes for your Playbook

- Nothing truly changes in an organization until the culture changes.
- Anthropology, the scientific study of humans, is primarily the result of observation.
- The culture is shaped by beliefs, customs, values, institutions, languages, inventions, even technology.
- Through enculturation, values and habits are passed on to succeeding generations.
- Every organization needs its own unique traditions and culture.
- In an enterprise, the culture is usually dominated by the informal organization.
- Companies, like societies, are held together by what the members have in common.

DISCIPLINE #9

MATHEMATICS

"Scientific" is not synonymous with quantification—
if it were, astrology would be the queen of the sciences.
– Peter Drucker

If you think a business can succeed on vision, inspiration, and passion alone, think again! When you get beyond the mission statement and leadership, and lift the lid on any enterprise, you will find numbers—hundreds, thousands, even millions of them.

Whether they like it or not, managers have to be able to crunch statistics. They can't leave that job to the "bean counters" and pretend it's outside their own portfolio.

As a leader in a corporation, there are basics you simply must have a handle on. They include matters such as sales forecasting, inventory management, price discounts, markups and markdowns, payroll calculations, consumer and business credit, compound interest, and financial analysis.

We are not saying you have to be a whiz at math, but it is essential that you know the fundamentals of fractions, decimals, percentages, and basic algebra.

The term "business math" is often referred to as "commercial math" or "consumer math" used in everyday life for practical applications. Thankfully, we have handy calculators and computers to do most of the work, but it is vital that we know what we're putting *in* so we can understand what is coming *out.*

Math and You

The person who says, "I just want to manage. I'm going to leave that math thing to someone else," is not living in the real world.

Whether consciously or unconsciously, the average person uses math every day—setting the alarm clock, stepping on the bathroom scales, or adjusting the thermometer. Sometimes you even try a few calculations that are a little more complicated. When driving, for example, you look at your speed, glance at your watch, and estimate the time you'll reach your destination.

On the job, we depend on math to design, develop and test products. It's how insurance companies calculate risks and know how much to charge for coverage.

But let's look at the subject personally. What about you? How confident are you concerning "numbers" when making decisions that affect your company or organization?

Bombarded With Data

As leaders and managers, almost daily we are handed

reams of data. What does it tell us? What should we do about it?

Since we work in a mine field of accounting statements income records, balance sheets, cash flow details, return on investment reports, and many more, mathematics becomes the key tool in understanding what they all mean.

There are many factors in the equation:

- How do the numbers from the factory floor relate to the numbers of the accountant?
- What is the difference in measuring information from a service environment vs. manufacturing?
- How can analytical reports be made understandable to the average employee?
- What are the key indicators used to track performance for your organization?
- How should you design an experiment that is worth the time and effort?
- What should you know when selecting effective charts and graphs?

The CEO, CFO, and their managers are being bombarded with more and more data. Does he/she know how to deal with the information when it is received? Interpreting the company math isn't an option, it is a necessity. Don't overlook the fact that "bad numbers will get you every time."

THE TIMELINE

Mathematics has been around much longer than most people realize. For example, in the G. A. Plimpton Collection at Columbia University is a tablet known as *Plimpton 322*. It is actually a Babylonian clay tablet believed to be written about 1800 BC, containing four columns and 15 rows of numbers used to solve mathematical problems.

We credit the early Chinese mathematics (11th century BC) with refining assigned values. Later, in the 6th century BC, the Pythagoreans in Greece, coined the term "mathematics" from the Greek *mathema*, which means "subject of instruction." Then came the application of deductive reasoning and "proofs" to the process.

We can thank the creation of the Hindu-Arabic numeral system and rules for its use (1st century AD) for what we still use today.

Down through the centuries, mathematics has played a significant role in the development of nations, the creation of inventions, and mass production—leading to the digital world that is exploding all around us:

- The "Age of Discovery," which began in the 15th century, allowed explorers to cross oceans by use of nautical charts and astronomical tables.
- Starting with Isaac Newton, the English physicist and mathematician, the Scientific Revolution was begun in the late 1600s.

- The Industrial Revolution was ushered in when James Watt, a Scottish mechanical engineer, created a steam engine with rotary motion (1765). He coined the word "horsepower" when calculating how his invention could replace the work of "x" number of horses.
- In the first half of the 1800s, mathematicians and engineers invented batteries, gas and electric lights, a steam-powered locomotive, the stethoscope, a sewing machine, the commercial reaper, and a mechanical calculator.
- By the end of the 19th century, the commercial world was buzzing with the invention of the rotary washing machine, man-made plastics, the telephone, motion pictures, a mechanical cash register, and the internal combustion engine.
- In 1903, the Wright brothers invented the first gas-motored, manned airplane. Five years later, the first Model-T Ford rolled off the assembly line. Later in the century came radar, helicopters, television, the atomic bomb, transistors, credit cards, bar codes, microchips, and the computer—perhaps the most significant invention of all.
- Now, in the 21st century, the world was introduced to the artificial heart, hybrid cars—and the amazing work of math-minded, creative people continues on.

THE BASICS

In reality, mathematics encompasses a group of sciences including arithmetic, algebra, geometry, calculus, etc., that deal with quantities, magnitudes, and forms, and their attributes and relationships by the use of symbols and numbers.

To break down the basics:

- *Arithmetic* concerns problems with numbers.
- *Algebra* involves equations in which letters represent unknown quantities.
- *Geometry* concerns the properties and relationships of figures in space.
- *Calculus*, a more complex form of math, allows us to find lengths, areas, and volumes.

These skills can help us solve some of the most serious puzzles we face. Since mathematics is based on logic, it usually starts from widely accepted statements and applies reasoning to draw conclusions.

The field is commonly divided into *pure mathematics* (advancing the knowledge for its own sake) and *applied mathematics* (developing math techniques for use in science, economics, and many other areas).

KEY CONCEPTS

In the MBA classes we have taught, we have seen how a group of students can "play dead" when they feel a topic is boring. But when the subject matter personally touches their lives, and they can visualize themselves working on a project involving the concept, suddenly the room is sparked with energy, expectation, and excitement.

We have seen this happen when we introduce concepts such as:

- QFD – Quality Function Deployment. This transforms the voice of the customer into engineering characteristics for a service or product.
- TRIZ – a problem-solving mechanism based on data, logic, and research. (The acronym is from its Russian inventor and doesn't translate well). Here's the basic idea. Someone, somewhere has already solved this problem (or one very similar), so you find that solution and creatively apply it to what you're working on.
- Six Sigma – The name comes from the goal of the manufacturer to have 99.99966% of the products to be free of defects. It was first introduced by Motorola in 1986 and widely adopted after Jack Welch made it the focus of his business strategy at General Electric a decade later.

- RPD – Robust Parameter Design. This was developed by a Japanese engineer, Genichi Taguchi. It distinguishes between factors you can control and those you can't when designing a product.

It is worth mentioning that the *Invention Machine's Goldfire* software (inspired by TRIZ) calls upon all the known knowledge from the physical and mathematical sciences [for instance physics, chemistry, biology, algebra, geometry, calculus, statistics, etc.] which allows us to resolve and place quantifiable probabilities on our design. We now have a high degree of assurance that what we have planned can meet the physical requirements. Of course we have to also think about systems to carry the work forward.

These concepts have the potential to open up a whole new world for creative companies. For example, by using the parameters that can be discovered with new technical tools, a product can be designed to endure the harshest of conditions—even in space or under the oceans.

CRUNCHING THE NUMBERS

We once again come face to face with Darwin's survival theory, which was presented to explain why certain animals or creatures have dominance over others. Herbert Spencer applied the theory in the late 1800s to explain why some industrial organizations survive and others don't.

Chester Barnard (a former New Jersey Bell president), in his classic book, *The Functions of the Executive*, writes that the singular function of the executive is to make sure that the organization survives.

Before the widespread use of computers, mathematical models coming out of the military operations research field from WW II were being used for decision making.

But today's availability to high speed computer access makes the *crunching of numbers* faster and easier than ever. However, understanding the significance still takes skill beyond the computer.

You only need to click on the website of Bloomburg or the Wall Street Journal to know that the stock market is a blur of numbers rather than a blast of words. Following and understanding what these numbers all mean is critical.

For years, business leaders have thrown around the term "Game Theory." It came into the business vocabulary in the mid-1940s and is still used in one form or another to the present day.

In essence, it is the study of strategic decision making, using mathematical models of conflict and cooperation between those making the choices.

One of the subjects it addresses is the concept of *zero-sum games*—meaning one person's gains equal exactly the net losses of the other participant(s). Over time, game theory has been applied to a very wide range of behaviors (both human and non-human), including animals and computers. You find it used in biology, political science, economics, even philosophy.

THE QUALITY MOVEMENT

The story of quality started with numbers and has ended up becoming something we now call *excellence* or *total customer satisfaction.* But the narrative began by studying variation—which involved collecting mountains of data in the form of numbers.

The first fifty years of the "quality movement" in this country (and later overseas), was carried on the back of understanding statistics, variation, and how to plot control charts, interpret normal curves, conduct tests of significance, and draw probability curves. It is the *hard stuff* that mathematicians and other technical people do.

However, quality eventually became a function in manufacturing that cut across departmental lines and required the cooperation of many departments. To be successful, it demanded a knowledge of systems thinking—which meant it needed the understanding, support, and commitment of management.

The first 50 years are now referred to as the years of the "Little Q." Now we have "Big Q"—*total quality management.* Once again we see the importance of relationships among all of the disciplines to achieve the goals of the organization.

In discussing the quality movement, reference is made to its impact on industry, but often overlooked is the success of W. Edwards Deming and Joseph M. Juran when they were invited to Japan after WW II to help transform that nation from a military power to an economic one.

KEEPING SCORE!

Getting a grasp on the numbers will allow you to test for significance from the data you collect from observations and other efforts. Plus, you will be able to measure, weigh and define past results and future goals.

Remember, there can be no game if you don't keep score!

An example of how statistics are being used to measure organizational success can be seen in the following illustration. If you look at overlapping bell curves and see an increase in overall performance, the difference is called "The Zone of Improvement."

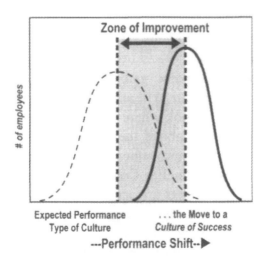

This is based on changing the culture and also applies to anthropology, where the improvement is gained by how people, internally, treat each other: "Your success is as important as my success."

LOOK FOR THE MEANING

A flyer came across our desk announcing a seminar titled: *Understanding Variation: The Key to Managing Chaos*. What stood out was the tag line, "Your performance, and the performance of your organization hinge on the accurate use and understanding of data."

The message was clear: we live in an information age, and much of that knowledge comes to us in the form of numbers. How true. Wherever we look, we are surrounded by ever-increasing mountains of statistics. But it is only useful when analyzed, interpreted, and assimilated in a meaningful way.

The traditional approach to analyzing routine data falls into two general categories: (1) comparisons to averages and (2) comparisons to specifications. However, neither approach can provide the essential information and insight you need to make reliable business decisions.

The seminar brochure also stated, "By missing vital information locked up in your monthly reports, you may be blissfully leading your company, department, or organization to disaster. Unless you know how to explore key data relationships, your decisions can have an adverse impact on profitability."

This lets us know how *alive* mathematics is—in many forms—in your organization every day!

Mathematics is a discipline of leadership that demands your addition, not your subtraction.

Notes for your Playbook

- Every leader needs to have a handle on business math.
- Interpreting company statistics is not an option, but a necessity.
- Bad numbers will get you every time.
- As a manager or leader you will be more concerned with applied math than pure math.
- Understand and utilize the key concepts of math that impact business today.
- Put the findings of the quality movement to work in your organization.
- Mathematics helps you keep score!
- Use the numbers to guide you to success.
- A total knowledge of your organization's data leads to profitability.

DISCIPLINE #10

COMMUNICATION

*I don't care how much a man
talks if he only says it in a few words.*
– Josh Billings

To most people, the word *manager* doesn't mean someone who does the labor, but a person who works with the workers. He or she does this in the form of expression, direction, etc., commonly known as *communication*.

This discipline has evolved more dramatically than any of the other behavioral sciences because it is so evident and obvious to us—from historic messengers on foot to today's incredible [no time lag] discourse by phone, computer, text messages, FaceTime or FaceBook, etc. It is both incredible, and at times a little scary. If we can see and talk to them; they in turn can see and talk to us!

In the most simple terms, communication is the exchange of thoughts, facts, and ideas—which are the link to innovation and progress.

The "Medium"

The arts of presentation, listening, advising, coaching and reaching understanding have entered a new world driven by technology and an insatiable desire to have everything available at the click of a mouse.

It is this instant communications ability, combined with more understanding of others' differences, that is supposed to keep us out of future world wars, as well as, help us conduct our organizational affairs on a global scale.

This exchange of information involves body language and other non-speaking signals. Since how well we communicate determines how well we manage, it is a skill that must be looked on as a lifelong learning tool and continuously improved upon. Our language skills need to be sharp enough so we can convey our messages without the need of interpreters.

Of the ten disciplines, communication, is the mechanism for all of the other relationships. It is through this "medium" that all else takes place—including negotiation, conflict resolution, and myriad parts of interaction between people.

For Better or Worse

In earlier times, managers could assemble, hoard, and disseminate information as they saw fit, often for their own benefit. Since we now have such wide access to data and facts, this is no longer the case.

A study of communication is a "book" on the technological advances that man has made over several thousands of years, which today are almost instantaneous. With current technology, there is no assurance that any individual, state, or country can carry out an activity that is not known by others. The accusations between major nations regarding "eavesdropping" on supposed secret conversations has risen to the highest levels.

Big Brother is truly at our doorstep—and we are not yet sure if it will be used for the common good or to inflict more human suffering. This is why many are asking, "Has our brain kept up with our information? Has our ability to gain wisdom paralleled our access to knowledge?"

Regardless of what the problem may be, or what has caused it, we usually hear the excuse, "Communications could have been better."

J. Lewis Powell, author of *Executive Speaking,* made this astute observation: "The prime purpose of speaking is to communicate ideas effectively; every other purpose is secondary. Grammar is a nicety, but is no more essential to communication than schooling is to education. You can be very grammatical and say nothing in a boring manner; or you can be very ungrammatical and very effective. When a truck driver bellows 'Get the hell out of the way' it may be poor grammar but it's effective communications."

THE MILESTONES

We've come a long way from the ancient world, when the

time span between sending a message to a distant country could stretch into months or even years.

Let's take a look at the communications milestones that have brought us to this present day:

- Prehistoric paintings have been found on the walls and ceilings of caves in France and Spain dating to 30,000 BC.
- The Phoenicians, in 1050 BC, developed the first alphabet based on sound—from which we have *phonetics.*
- In 776 BC, the first recorded use of homing pigeons were used to send messages of the winners of the Olympic Games to the Athenians.
- The Chinese wrote on silk, wood, and bamboo as early as 400 BC.
- In 200 BC, human messengers on foot or horseback (with relay stations) were common in Egypt and China.
- The recorded history of American Indians includes how they used smoke signals to communicate danger, victory, or to call gatherings.
- In 1000 AD, the Mayans in Yucatan, Mexico, made writing paper from tree bark.
- Soon after the invention of movable type printing, newspapers began to appear in Europe in 1460.
- In 1661, postal service was begun in the colony of Virginia.

- Gugliemo Marconi transmitted radio signals across the Atlantic Ocean in 1702.
- In 1714, the first typewriter appeared in England.
- Samuel Morse invented the Morse code in 1843, communicating to amateur radio operators using dots and dashes.
- The Pony Express was established in 1860 to carry mail by horseback from Saint Joseph, Missouri, to Sacramento, California (changing horses about every 10 miles). A letter from New York could reach the West Coast in 10 days.
- Alexander Graham Bell invented the electric telephone in 1876.
- In 1885, George Eastman patented the Kodak roll film camera.
- The first radio station, KDKA in Pittsburgh, Pennsylvania, hit the airways in 1920.
- 1927, Vladimir Zworykin invented a television camera. The first commercial television station, WNBT (now WNBC), began broadcasting in New York City in 1941.
- Computers were first sold commercially in 1951.
- In 1994, the United States government released control of the Internet and the www—World Wide Web—was born.

MOVING THE MESSAGE

Today's high-speed digital world has drastically changed

how problems are solved. In the "old days"—which we can now claim to be just a couple of decades ago—we moved messages in business primarily by in-house meetings or small-group conferences. This was sometimes known as the forum of management, where they behave like early philosophers —discussing much, deciding little.

The current speed and access to issues has caused some dramatic power shifts. For example, the Chinese government is finding it harder and harder to keep information buried in the sand.

Because of Skype, GoToMeeting.com, and other digital platforms, we have live, interactive discussions with participants joining in from all corners of the globe.

Even more, a call may go out for input on some issue and responses flood in from everywhere. One executive smiled and said, "We have seen the light and Twitter has set us free."

Something amazing has been taking place in organizations from Oslo to Osaka. For the first time in history, the messenger is the one who is making the "big bucks." We are talking about the Information Technology specialists who are absolutely essential in keeping communications flowing.

Young, skilled, computer engineers are in short supply. Remember the first law of economics—the law of supply and demand? Take a look at national "job openings" and you'll find that companies are willing to offer a competent IT guy or gal almost anything to come on board. Others in the workforce may call them "spoiled brats," but so what?

Without them, an organization can't keep up with the competition.

What these young people are bringing to the current Age of Knowledge is not knowledge, but the skill of directing others how to more easily find this information (i.e., Internet, software programs, etc.).

It has been a rude awakening for older workers who believe their experience should have high monetary value. Yet, that's not the case. It seems their "knowledge" has been siphoned from them and is now digitized and stored in a cyberspace "cloud" for everyone else's use. The person who can help you find it is the individual who is cashing in.

As we write this, the market value of Google is $386 *billion*. From its search engine you can find out what the late Abraham Maslow had to say about psychology, which for the most part does not benefit his heirs to any significant degree.

This didn't happen when Johannes Gutenberg invented the printing press in 1445. The workers who were getting blacked from the print did not become millionaires.

Computers don't actually think, but they come mighty close to it in the way they can arrange all sorts of inputs in an incredibly short period of time. Perhaps you remember when "Big Blue" defeated World Chess Champion Garry Kasparov in 1997. Today, these "man vs. machine" matches are almost always won by the computer. After all, they can search as many as 200 million chess positions per *second!*

BASIC DESIRES

There is a strong tie between the disciplines of psychology and communication. It has often been said that humans are herd animals and that the chief duty of the CEO is to "stay connected." When he/she doesn't, there will be consequences.

Jonathan D. Port, a quality engineer and author, has listed seven basic "desires" that people seek:

Desire #1: To be heard and understood
Desire #2: To be affirmed
Desire #3: To be blessed
Desire #4: To be safe
Desire #5: To be touched
Desire #6: To be chosen
Desire #7: To be included

If the men and women you lead are looking for these same results, what are you doing to provide their needs? In what areas can you improve?

ONE-TO-ONE

While emails, text messages, and voice mail have their place, nothing compares with face-to-face personal communication. Anything else is second rate by comparison.

Lawrence King, president of King Strategic Alliance in

California, believes every business leader (CEO) needs to utilize one-to-one personalized coaching with each of his/her managers. He recommends:

- Schedule protected quality time each month of at least one hour per manager.
- Keep the discussion meaningful and lively, participating with energy and enthusiasm.
- Let the manager know in advance what issues will be addressed in the one-to-one.
- The CEO should ask good opening questions, forcing the manager to think in different ways about the issues.
- The CEO probes for critical business opportunities and problems.
- Action plans are developed and reviewed by the CEO and manager in the one-to-ones.
- Plan to spend at least 25% of the time discussing long-term strategic issues.
- Talk over how the one-to-ones are working and how they could be improved.

COMMUNICATORS WHO CARE

While private conversations are beneficial, there are times when the discussion needs to expand beyond just two people.

For example, when an issue arises in the workplace that affects a number of employees, it's not enough for just one or two individuals to sit in a corner and attempt to find a solution. At the very minimum, a team needs to be appointed—representing a cross-section of the hierarchy—to confront the sticking point.

The first task is to carefully define the true problem, and then have total agreement that "this is the issue!"

Once this is accomplished, allow a time period for clarifying questions. Everyone should have an opportunity to probe all aspects to gain as much knowledge as possible. Only after stating the problem succinctly and supplying enough supporting information can you begin to seek solutions.

If the situation at hand is broad rather than narrow, the solution may need to be divided into several categories. This may require brainstorming to enlist input from all parties to build the subdivisions that form the system—which supports the problem we are working on.

Placing the data into categories allows us to break the system down into components and study each one individually. Other tools, such as flow charts, check sheets, fishbone diagrams, and matrices provide us with ways to analyze the information.

This approach allows us to test and work on the basic system and avoid assigning random blame.

The "Fishbone" cause and effect diagram, developed by Kaoru Ishikawa during his tenure at the Kawasaki shipyards in Japan is an effective brainstorming tool that helps identify barriers to success that need to be addressed and adjusted.

A SAMPLE ISHIKAWA "FISHBONE"

Timely communication can dispel rumors and misconceptions. The best rule is to either tell the truth or nothing at all.

It's sad but true that lying has become our nation's number one illness—and in business it often starts at the top. To many, deceit has become an acceptable way of life, but it is like a cancer that eats away at confidence and trust.

Every leader should remove the barriers to understanding by being authentic and being available. There is no better way to build a loyal workforce than to show you care.

In this book, communication may be listed as the tenth discipline, but it has the power to make the other nine truly awaken and come to life. That's why we encourage you to master this art and daily put it into practice.

Notes for your Playbook

- Communication, the exchange of thoughts, facts, and ideas, is basic to human progress.
- Instant information technology has revolutionized how business is conducted.
- Computer and IT experts are among an organization's most valued and highest paid employees.
- There are strong ties between communication and the other disciplines.
- Every CEO needs to learn the art of having one-to-one meetings with his/her managers.
- When addressing group problems, first have total agreement on the issue before seeking solutions.
- The best way to build a loyal workforce is to communicate how much you care.

FROM PLAYBOOK TO PERFORMANCE

Now it's your turn.

As a result of examining the principles found on these pages, we trust you have the big picture of how each distinct area of knowledge interrelates and impacts you and your organization.

With this knowledge, start designing your own plays and test them in the real world. You'll soon discover that the keys to business and personal success are found in *The Ten Disciplines of Leadership.*

References and Recommended Reading

Discipline #1: Psychology

Blanchard, Ken; Hersey, Paul; Johnson, Dewey, *Management of Organizational Behavior – Utilizing Human Resources,* Prentice-Hall, 1996.

Brown, J. Douglas, *The Human Nature of Organizations,* AMACON, 1973.

Csikszentmihalyi, Mihaly, *Flow: The Psychology of Optimal Experience,* Harper, 1990.

Dewey, John, *Human Nature and Conduct,* Henry Holt and Co., 1922.

Harris, Thomas A. *I'm OK – You're OK: A Practical Guide to Transactional Analysis,* Harper & Row, 1967.

Jaques, Elliott, *Requisite Organization,* Cason Hall & Co., 2006.

Leman, Kevin, *When Your Best in Not Good Enough*, Fleming H. Revell, 1988.

Maslow, A. H., *The Farther Reaches of Human Nature*, Viking Press, 1971.

Maslow, A.H., *Maslow on Management,* John Wiley & Sons, 1998

Maslow, A. H., *Motivation and Personality*, Harper & Brothers, 1954.

McGregor, Douglas, *Leadership and Motivation* (Essays), M.I.T. Press, 1966.

McGregor, Douglas, *The Human Side of Enterprise*, McGraw-Hill, 1960, 1985.

Peale, Norman Vincent, *The Power of Positive Thinking,* Prentice-Hall, 1952.

Skinner, B.F., *About Behaviorism,* Alfred A. Knopf, 1974.

Skinner, B. F., *Science and Human Behavior,* Macmillan, 1953.

Discipline #2: Sociology

Deal, Terrence; Kennedy, Alan, *Corporate Cultures: The Rites and Ritual of Corporate Life,* Basic Books, 2000.

Goodwin, Doris Kearns, *A Team of Rivals,* Simon & Schuster, 2006.

Harvey, Jerry B., *How Come Every Time I Get Stabbed in the Back My Fingerprints Are on the Knife? (and Other Meditations on Management),* Jossey-Bass, 1999.

Himes, Joseph H., *The Study of Sociology,* Scott, Foresman & Co., 1968.

Jaques, Elliott, *Requisite Organization: A Total System for Effective Managerial Organization and Managerial Leadership for the 21st Century,* Cason Hall Publishers, 1996.

Katzenbach, Jon R.; Smith, Douglas K., *The Wisdom of Teams: Creating the High-Performance Organization,* Harper Business, 1993.

Kayser, Thomas A., *Team Power: How to Unleash the Collaborative Genius of Work Teams,* Irwin, 1994.

Kotkin, Joel, *Tribes: How Race, Religion, and Identity Determine Success in the New Global Economy,* Random House, 1994.

Larsen, Otto N.; Lundberg, George A.; Schrag, Clarence C., *Sociology,* Harper & Row, 1963.

Lewin, Kurt, *Resolving Social Conflicts,* American Psychological Association, 1997.

Mann, Michael, *Workers on the Move: The Sociology of Relocation,* Cambridge University Press, 1973.

Discipline #3: Philosophy

Beauchanmp, Tom L., *Philosophical Ethics: An Introduction to Moral Philosophy,* McGraw-Hill, 1982.

Blanchard, Ken; O'Connor, Michael, *Managing By Values,* Berrett-Koehler Publishers, 1997.

DeBono, Edward, *Six Thinking Hats,* Little, Brown, and Company, Revised Edition, 1999.

DeBono, Edward, *DeBono's Thinking Course,* Facts on File, Inc. Revised Edition, 1994.

Drucker, Peter F., *The Essential Drucker: The Best of Sixty Years of Peter Drucker's Essential Writings on Management,* Harper Business, 2001.

Durant, Will, *The Story of Philosophy,* Washington Square Press, 1961.

Dygert, Charles B.; Jacobs, Richard A., *Managing for Success,* Motivational Enterprises, 1997.

Meyers, Gerald E., *The Spirit of American Philosophy,* Putnam's, 1970.

Reid, John, *A Theory of Value,* Scribener's Sons, 1938.

Vaill, Peter B., *Managing as a Performing Art,* Jossey-Bass, 1989.

Discipline #4: Geography

Downs, Roger M. and Mahler, Scott, *National Geographic Almanac of Geography,* National Geographic Society, 2005.

Holt-Jensen, Arild, *Geography: History and Concepts,* SAGE Publications, 2009.

Fenneman, Nevin M., *The Circumference of Geography*, Association of American Geographers ,1919.

Discipline #5: History

Cochran, Thomas C, and Miller, William, *The Age of Enterprise—A Social History of America,* Harper & Row, 1942, 1961.

Cooper, Robert K., Ayman, Sawaf, *Emotional EQ: Emotional Intelligence in Leadership and Organization,* Grosset/Putnam, 1996.

Drucker, Peter F., *The New Realities: In Government and Politics/In Economics and Business / In Society and World View,* Harper & Row, 1989.

Fandt, Patricia M., Goodman, Stephen H., and Lewis, Pamela S., *Management: Challenges for the 21st Century,* South-Western College Publishing, 1998.

Orwell, George, *Animal Farm* (50th Annivesary Edition), Signet, 1996.

Zunz, Oliver (Ed.), *Reliving the Past: The Worlds of Social History,* University of North Carolina Press, 1985.

Discipline #6: Political Science

Dilenschneider, Robert L., *Power and Influence*, McGraw-Hill, 2007.

Greene, Robert, *The 48 Laws of Power,* Viking, 1998.

Klein, Gary, *Sources of Power: How People Make Decisions,* MIT Press, 2001.

Kotter, John P., *Power in Management,* AMACON Publications, 1979.

Machiavelli, Niccolo, *The Prince*, Penguin Classics, 2003.

Markle, Garold L., *Catalytic Coaching: The End of the Performance Review,* Praeger, 2000.

Stauss, Leo, *History of Political Philosophy,* University of Chicago Press,1987.

Discipline #7: Economics

Galbraith, John Kenneth, *The Age of Uncertainty – A History of Economic Ideas and their Consequences,* Houghton Mifflin, 1977.

Heilbroner, Robert L., *The Worldly Philosophers: The Lives, Times, and Ideas of the Great Economic Thinkers,* Simon & Schuster, 1953.

Keiser, Norman F., *Economics: Analysis and Policy*, John Wiley & Sons, 1965.

Kotkin, Joel, *Tribes: How Race, Religion, and Identity Determine Success in the New Global Economy*, Random House, 1994.

Marx, Karl, *Capital: Critique of Political Economy*, Penguin Classics, 1992.

Nordhaus, William D., and Samuelson, Paul A., *Economics*, McGraw-Hill, 1989.

Discipline #8: Anthropology

Goversmith, Frank, *Class, Culture, and Social Change: A New View of the 1930s*, Harvester Press, Sussex (UK), 1980.

Harris, Marvin, *Culture, Man, and Nature: An Introduction to General Anthropology*, Crowell, 1971.

Jacobs, Melville and Stern, Bernhard, *Outline of Anthropology*, Barnes & Noble, 1947.

Leman, Kevin, *The Birth Order Book*, Dell, 1985.

Discipline #9: Mathematics

Bernard, Chester I., *The Functions of the Executive: 30th Anniversary Edition*, Harvard University Press, 1971.

Boyer, Carl B., and Merzbach, Uta C., *A History of Mathematics*, Wiley, 2011.

Clendenen, Gary, and Salzman, Stanley A., *Business Mathematics*, Pearson, 2014.

Kramers, Kraig, *CEO Tools: The Nuts-N-Bolts of Business for Every Manager's Success*, Gandy Dancer Press, 2002

Shao, Lawrence P. and Shao, Stephen, *Mathematics for Management and Finance*, Thomson Publishing, 1997.

Discipline #10: Communication

Lipman-Bluman, Jean, *The Connective Edge: Leading in an Interdependent World*, Jossey-Bass, 1996.

Port, Jonathan D., "7 Ways to Enhance Workplace Relationships, Motivation, and Productivity," *Quality Progress*, July, 2013.

Powell, J. Lewis, *Executive Speaking: An Acquired Skill*, BNA Inc., 1972.

Scott, Susan, *Fierce Conversations: Achieving Success at Work and in Life, One Conversation at a Time*, Viking, 2002

WITH DEEP APPRECIATION

Special Thanks from Rich Jacobs to the dozens of TEC/Vistage Speakers—1999-2015—who presented ideas and challenged me and my members with many of the concepts appearing in this book. It is impossible to single out several speakers without missing the names of some others, but special appreciation goes to:

Pat Murray: Essence of Leadership and Group Dynamics
    (the "essence" of Vistage)
Don Schmincke: The Code of the Executive
Jack Kaine: Negotiations
Michael Allosso: Presentation and Communication Skills
Adrian Geering: CEO and Managers as Coaches
Jim Alampi: Execution, Strategic Planning, Five Dysfunctions
Tom Foster: Who is Elliott Jaques? – Time Horizons
John Asher: Sales Management
Brian & Alan Beaulieu: Economics, Forecasting and what is
    next
Susan Scott: Fierce Conversations
Kraig Kramers: CEO Toolkit
Criag Weber: Communications
Dan Barnett: Executive (Your Make or Break)
Shawn Ishler: Temperament Counts
Herb Meyer: What's Happening Globally
Carloz Rizowy: Global Trends
Ole Carlson: Inside TEC
James Newton: Visionary Leadership
Jack Daly: Sales
Gerry Layo: Sales
Edgar Papke: Alignment
Michael Canic: Consistency
Boaz Rauchwerger: "Unbelievable"!
Steven Snyder: Finding Your Quiet Place
John Schuster: Master Coaching

Tom Hill: A New Way of Thinking and Linking Up
Roger Blackwell: Saving America
Ton Searcy: Whale Hunting
Mike Matalone: Hiring and Retaining Top Talent
Howard Hyden: Think Strategically and Other Good Advice
Dave Nelson: Social Media
Gini Dietrich: Social Media
Steve Anderson: Reflection – How Do We Improve?
Hunter Lott: Human Resources
Mark Wiskup: Communications
Rick Houcek: Strategic Planning

A SPECIAL THANKS TO THE CURRENT COLUMBUS CHAIRS

Glenn Waring: Senior Chair speaker on Finance for 20 years
Ken Ackerman: logistics and warehousing expert, author of
    many books on the subject
Artie Isaac: Vistage Rookie Chair of 2012 and Innovation
    Speaker of 2013
Joe Lorenz: former TEC member, and current Vistage Chair
    — and many more incredible speakers

FOR ADDITIONAL RESOURCES
BY THE AUTHORS
CONTACT:

RICHARD A. JACOBS
1705 DRY CREEK ROAD NE
GRANVILLE, OH 43023
EMAIL: richjacobs75@gmail.com